THE
SACRED
AND
THE
PROFANE

THE NATURE OF RELIGION

THE SACRED AND THE PROFANE

THE NATURE OF RELIGION

by Mircea Eliade

Translated from the French
by Willard R. Trask

A Harvest Book • Harcourt, Inc.
Orlando   Austin   New York   San Diego   Toronto   London

For information about permission to reproduce selections from this book,
write to Permissions, Houghton Mifflin Harcourt Publishing Company,
215 Park Avenue South, New York, New York 10003.

www.hmhco.com

ISBN-13: 978-0-15-679201-1 (pb)
ISBN-10: 0-15-679201-X (pb)
Library of Congress Catalog Card Number: 58-10904

Printed in the United States of America
DOC 50 49 48

CONTENTS

INTRODUCTION

The extraordinary interest aroused all over the world by Rudolf Otto's *Das Heilige* (The Sacred), published in 1917, still persists. Its success was certainly due to the author's new and original point of view. Instead of studying the *ideas* of God and religion, Otto undertook to analyze the modalities of *the religious experience*. Gifted with great psychological subtlety, and thoroughly prepared by his twofold training as theologian and historian of religions, he succeeded in determining the content and specific characteristics of religious experience. Passing over the rational and speculative side of religion, he concentrated chiefly on its irrational aspect. For Otto had read Luther and had understood what the "living God" meant to a believer. It was not the God of the philosophers—of Erasmus, for example; it was not an idea, an abstract notion, a mere moral allegory. It was a terrible *power*, manifested in the divine wrath.

In *Das Heilige* Otto sets himself to discover the characteristics of this frightening and irrational experience. He finds the *feeling of terror* before the sacred, before the awe-inspiring mystery (*mysterium tremendum*), the majesty (*majestas*) that emanates an overwhelming superiority of power; he finds *religious fear* before the fascinating mystery (*mysterium fascinans*) in which perfect fullness of being flowers. Otto characterizes all these experiences as numinous (from Latin *numen*, god), for they are induced by the revelation of an aspect of divine power. The numinous presents itself as something "wholly other" (*ganz andere*), something basically and totally different. It is like nothing human or cosmic; confronted with it, man senses his profound nothingness, feels that he is only a creature, or, in the words in which Abraham addressed the Lord, is "but dust and ashes" (Genesis, 18, 27).

The sacred always manifests itself as a reality of a wholly different order from "natural" realities. It is true that language naively expresses the *tremendum*, or the *majestas*, or the *mysterium fascinans* by terms borrowed from the world of nature or from man's secular mental life. But we know that this analogical terminology is due precisely to human inability to express the *ganz andere*; all that goes beyond man's natural experience, language is reduced to suggesting by terms taken from that experience.

After forty years, Otto's analyses have not lost their value; readers of this book will profit by reading and reflecting on them. But in the following pages we adopt a different perspective. We propose to present the phenomenon of the sacred in all its complexity, and not only in so far as it is *irrational*. What will concern us is not the relation between the rational and nonrational elements of religion but the *sacred in its entirety*. The first possible definition of the *sacred* is that it is *the opposite of the profane*. The aim of the following pages is to illustrate and define this opposition between sacred and profane.

WHEN THE SACRED MANIFESTS ITSELF

Man becomes aware of the sacred because it manifests itself, shows itself, as something wholly different from the profane. To designate the *act of manifestation* of the sacred, we have proposed the term *hierophany*. It is a fitting term, because it does not imply anything further; it expresses no more than is implicit in its etymological content, *i.e.*, that *something sacred shows itself to us*.[1] It could be said that the history of religions—from the most primitive to the most highly developed—is constituted by a great number of hierophanies, by manifestations of sacred realities. From the most elementary hierophany—*e.g.*, manifestation of the sacred in some ordinary object, a stone or a tree—to the supreme hierophany (which, for a Christian, is the incarnation of God in Jesus Christ) there is no solution of continuity. In each case we are confronted by the same mysterious act—the manifestation of something of a wholly different order, a reality that does not belong to our world, in objects that are an integral part of our natural "profane" world.

The modern Occidental experiences a certain uneasiness before many manifestations of the sacred. He finds it difficult to accept the fact that, for many human beings, the sacred can be manifested in stones or trees, for

[1] Cf. Mircea Eliade, *Patterns in Comparative Religion*, New York, Sheed & Ward, 1958, pp. 7 ff. Cited hereafter as *Patterns*.

example. But as we shall soon see, what is involved is not a veneration of the stone in itself, a cult of the tree in itself. The sacred tree, the sacred stone are not adored as stone or tree; they are worshipped precisely because they are *hierophanies*, because they show something that is no longer stone or tree but the *sacred*, the *ganz andere*.

It is impossible to overemphasize the paradox represented by every hierophany, even the most elementary. By manifesting the sacred, any object becomes *something else*, yet it continues to remain *itself*, for it continues to participate in its surrounding cosmic milieu. A *sacred* stone remains a *stone*; apparently (or, more precisely, from the profane point of view), nothing distinguishes it from all other stones. But for those to whom a stone reveals itself as sacred, its immediate reality is transmuted into a supernatural reality. In other words, for those who have a religious experience all nature is capable of revealing itself as cosmic sacrality. The cosmos in its entirety can become a hierophany.

The man of the archaic societies tends to live as much as possible *in* the sacred or in close proximity to consecrated objects. The tendency is perfectly understandable, because, for primitives as for the man of all premodern societies, the *sacred* is equivalent to a *power*, and, in the last analysis, to *reality*. The sacred is saturated with *being*. Sacred power means reality and at the same time enduringness and efficacity. The polarity sacred-profane is often expressed as an opposition between *real* and *unreal* or pseudoreal. (Naturally, we must not expect to find the archaic languages in possession of this philosophical terminology, *real-unreal*, etc.; but we find the *thing*.) Thus it is easy to understand that religious man deeply desires *to be*, to participate in *reality*, to be saturated with power.

Our chief concern in the following pages will be to elucidate this subject—to show in what ways religious man attempts to remain as long as possible in a sacred universe, and hence what his total experience of life proves to be in comparison with the experience of the man without religious feeling, of the man who lives, or wishes to live, in a desacralized world. It should be said at once that the *completely* profane world, the wholly desacralized cosmos, is a recent discovery in the history of the human spirit. It does not devolve upon us to show by what historical processes and as the result of what changes in spiritual attitudes and behavior modern man has desacralized his world and assumed a profane existence. For our purpose it is enough to observe that desacralization pervades the entire experience of the nonreligious man of modern societies and that, in consequence, he finds it increasingly difficult to rediscover the existential dimensions of religious man in the archaic societies.

TWO MODES OF BEING IN THE WORLD

The abyss that divides the two modalities of experience—sacred and profane—will be apparent when we come to describe sacred space and the ritual building of the human habitation, or the varieties of the religious experience of time, or the relations of religious man to nature and the world of tools, or the consecration of human life itself, the sacrality with which man's vital functions (food, sex, work and so on) can be charged. Simply calling to mind what the city or the house, nature, tools, or work have become for modern and nonreligious man will show with the utmost vividness all that distinguishes such a man from a man belonging to any archaic society, or even from a peasant of Christian Europe. For modern consciousness, a physiological act —eating, sex, and so on—is in sum only an organic phenomenon, however much it may still be encumbered by tabus (imposing, for example, particular rules for "eating properly" or forbidding some sexual behavior disapproved by social morality). But for the primitive, such an act is never simply physiological; it is, or can become, a sacrament, that is, a communion with the sacred.

The reader will very soon realize that *sacred* and *profane* are two modes of being in the world, two existential situations assumed by man in the course of his history. These modes of being in the world are not of concern only to the history of religions or to sociology; they are not the object only of historical, sociological, or ethnological study. In the last analysis, the *sacred* and *profane* modes of being depend upon the different positions that man has conquered in the cosmos; hence they are of concern both to the philosopher and to anyone seeking to discover the possible dimensions of human existence.

It is for this reason that, though he is a historian of religions, the author of this book proposes not to confine himself only to the perspective of his particular science. The man of the traditional societies is admittedly a *homo religiosus*, but his behavior forms part of the general behavior of mankind and hence is of concern to philosophical anthropology, to phenomenology, to psychology.

The better to bring out the specific characteristics of life in a world capable of becoming sacred, I shall not hesitate to cite examples from many religions belonging to different periods and cultures. Nothing can take the place of the example, the concrete fact. It would be useless to discuss the structure of sacred space without showing, by particular examples, how such a space is constructed and why it becomes qualitatively different from the profane space by which it is surrounded. I shall select such examples from among the Mesopotamians, the Indians, the Chinese, the Kwakiutl and other primitive peoples. From the historico-cultural point of view, such a juxtaposition of religious data pertaining to peoples so far removed in time and space is not without some danger. For there is always the risk of falling back into the errors of the nineteenth century and, particularly, of believing with Tylor or Frazer that the reaction of the human mind to natural phenomena is uniform. But the progress accomplished in cultural ethnology and in the history of religions has shown that this is not always true, that man's reactions to nature are often conditioned by his culture and hence, finally, by history.

But the important thing for our purpose is to bring out the specific characteristics of the religious experience, rather than to show its numerous variations and the differences caused by history. It is somewhat as if, in order to obtain a better grasp of the poetic phenomenon, we should have recourse to a mass of heterogeneous examples, and, side by side with Homer and Dante, quote Hindu, Chinese, and Mexican poems; that is, should take into consideration not only poetics possessing a historical common denominator (Homer, Vergil, Dante) but also creations that are dependent upon other esthetics. From the point of view of literary history, such juxtapositions are to be viewed with suspicion; but they are valid if our object is to describe the poetic phenomenon as such, if we propose to show the essential difference between poetic language and the utilitarian language of everyday life.

THE SACRED AND HISTORY

Our primary concern is to present the specific dimensions of religious experience, to bring out the differences between it and profane experience of the world. I shall not dwell on the variations that religious experience of the world has undergone in the course of time. It is obvious, for example, that the symbolisms and cults of Mother Earth, of human and agricultural fertility, of the sacrality of woman, and the like, could not develop and constitute a complex religious system except through the discovery of agriculture; it is equally obvious that a preagricultural society, devoted to hunting, could not feel the sacrality of Mother Earth in the same way or with the same intensity. Hence there are differences in religious experience explained by differences in economy, culture, and social organization—in short, by history. Nevertheless, between the nomadic hunters and the sedentary cultivators there is a similarity in behavior that seems to us infinitely more important than their differences: *both live in a sacralized cosmos*, both share in a cosmic sacrality manifested equally in the animal world and in the vegetable world. We need only compare their existential situations with that of a man of the modern societies, *living in a desacralized cosmos*, and we shall immediately be aware of all that separates him from them. At the same time we realize the validity of comparisons between religious facts pertaining to different cultures; all these facts arise from a single type of behavior, that of *homo religiosus*.

This little book, then, may serve as a general introduction to the history of religions, since it describes the modalities of the sacred and the situation of man in a world charged with religious values. But it is not a study in the history of religions in the strict sense, for the writer, in citing examples, has not undertaken to indicate their historico-cultural contexts. To do so would have required a work in several volumes. The reader will find all requisite information in the books listed in the Bibliography.

MIRCEA ELIADE

Saint-Cloud
April, 1956

CHAPTER 1

Sacred Space

and Making

the World Sacred

HOMOGENEITY OF SPACE AND HIEROPHANY

For religious man, space is not homogeneous; he experiences interruptions, breaks in it; some parts of space are qualitatively different from others. "Draw not nigh hither," says the Lord to Moses; "put off thy shoes from off thy feet, for the place whereon thou standest is holy ground" (Exodus, 3, 5). There is, then, a sacred space, and hence a strong, significant space; there are other spaces that are not sacred and so are without structure or consistency, amorphous. Nor is this all. For religious man, this spatial nonhomogeneity finds expression in the experience of an opposition between space that is sacred—the only *real* and *real-ly* existing space— and all other space, the formless expanse surrounding it.

It must be said at once that the religious experience of the nonhomogeneity of space is a primordial experience, homologizable to a founding of the world. It is not a matter of theoretical speculation, but of a primary religious experience that precedes all reflection on the world. For it is the break effected in space that allows the world to be constituted, because it reveals the fixed point, the central axis for all future orientation. When the sacred manifests itself in any hierophany, there is not only a break in the homogeneity of space; there is also revelation of an absolute reality, opposed to the nonreality of the vast surrounding expanse. The manifestation of the sacred ontologically founds the world. In the homogeneous and infinite expanse, in which no point of reference is possible and hence no *orientation* can be established, the hierophany reveals an absolute fixed point, a center.

So it is clear to what a degree the discovery—that is, the revelation—of a sacred space possesses existential value for religious man; for nothing can begin, nothing can be *done*, without a previous orientation—and any orientation implies acquiring a fixed point. It is for this reason that religious man has always sought to fix his abode at the "center of the world." *If the world is to be lived in*, it must be *founded*—and no world can come to birth in the chaos of the homogeneity and relativity of profane space. The discovery or projection of a fixed point—the center—is equivalent to the creation of the world; and we shall soon give some examples that will unmistakably show the cosmogonic value of the ritual orientation and construction of sacred space.

For profane experience, on the contrary, space is homogeneous and neutral; no break qualitatively differentiates the various parts of its mass. Geometrical space can be cut and delimited in any direction; but no qualitative differentiation and, hence, no orientation are given by virtue of its inherent structure. We need only remember how a classical geometrician defines space. Naturally, we must not confuse the *concept* of homogeneous and neutral geometrical space with the *experience* of profane space, which is in direct contrast to the experience of sacred space and which alone concerns our investigation. The *concept* of homogeneous space and the history of the concept (for it has been part of the common stock of philosophical and scientific thought since antiquity) are a wholly different problem, upon which we shall not enter here. What matters for our purpose is the *experience* of space known to nonreligious man— that is, to a man who rejects the sacrality of the world, who accepts only a profane existence, divested of all religious presuppositions.

It must be added at once that such a profane existence is never found in the pure state. To whatever degree he may have desacralized the world, the man who has made his choice in favor of a profane life never succeeds in completely doing away with religious behavior. This will become clearer as we proceed; it will appear that even the most desacralized existence still preserves traces of a religious valorization of the world.

But for the moment we will set aside this aspect of the problem and confine ourselves to comparing the two experiences in question—that of sacred space and that of profane space. The implications of the former experience have already been pointed out. Revelation of a sacred space makes it possible to obtain a fixed point and hence to acquire orientation in the chaos of homogeneity, to "found the world" and to live in a real sense. The profane experience, on the contrary, maintains the homogeneity and hence the relativity of space. No *true* orientation is now possible, for the fixed point no longer enjoys a unique ontological status; it appears and disappears in accordance with the needs of the day. Properly speaking, there is no longer any world, there are only fragments of a shattered universe, an amorphous mass consisting of an infinite number of more or less neutral places in which man moves, governed and driven by the obligations of an existence incorporated into an industrial society.

Yet this experience of profane space still includes values that to some extent recall the nonhomogeneity peculiar to the religious experience of space. There are, for example, privileged places, qualitatively different from all others—a man's birthplace, or the scenes of his first love, or certain places in the first foreign city he visited in youth. Even for the most frankly nonreligious man, all these places still retain an exceptional, a unique quality; they are the "holy places" of his private universe, as if it were in such spots that he had received the revelation of a reality *other* than that in which he participates through his ordinary daily life.

This example of crypto-religious behavior on profane man's part is worth noting. In the course of this book we shall encounter other examples of this sort of degradation and desacralization of religious values and forms of behavior. Their deeper significance will become apparent later.

THEOPHANIES AND SIGNS

To exemplify the nonhomogeneity of space as experienced by nonreligious man, we may turn to any religion. We will choose an example that is accessible to everyone—a church in a modern city. For a believer, the church shares in a different space from the street in which it stands. The door that opens on the interior of the church actually signifies a solution of continuity. The threshold that separates the two spaces also indicates the distance between two modes of being, the profane and the religious. The threshold is the limit, the boundary, the frontier that distinguishes and opposes two worlds—and at the same time the paradoxical place where those worlds communicate, where passage from the profane to the sacred world becomes possible.

A similar ritual function falls to the threshold of the human habitation, and it is for this reason that the threshold is an object of great importance. Numerous rites accompany passing the domestic threshold—a bow, a prostration, a pious touch of the hand, and so on. The threshold has its guardians—gods and spirits who forbid entrance both to human enemies and to demons and the powers of pestilence. It is on the threshold that sacrifices to the guardian divinities are offered. Here too certain palaeo-oriental cultures (Babylon, Egypt, Israel) situated the judgment place. The threshold, the door *show* the solution of continuity in space immediately and concretely; hence their great religious importance, for they are symbols and at the same time vehicles of *passage* from the one space to the other.

What has been said will make it clear why the church shares in an entirely different space from the buildings that surround it. Within the sacred precincts the profane world is transcended. On the most archaic levels of culture this possibility of transcendence is expressed by various *images of an opening*; here, in the sacred enclosure, communication with the gods is made possible; hence there must be a door to the world above, by which the gods can descend to earth and man can symbolically ascend to heaven. We shall soon see that this was the case in many religions; properly speaking, the temple constitutes an opening in the upward direction and ensures communication with the world of the gods.

Every sacred space implies a hierophany, an irruption of the sacred that results in detaching a territory from the surrounding cosmic milieu and making it qualitatively different. When Jacob in his dream at Haran saw a ladder reaching to heaven, with angels ascending and descending on it, and heard the Lord speaking from above it, saying: "I am the Lord God of Abraham," he awoke and was afraid and cried out: "How dreadful is this place: this is none other but the house of God, and this is the gate of heaven." And he took the stone that had been his pillow, and set it up as a monument, and poured oil on the top of it. He called the place Beth-el, that is, house of God (Genesis, 28, 12-19). The symbolism implicit in the expression "gate of heaven" is rich and complex; the theophany that occurs in a place consecrates it by the very fact that it makes it open above—that is, in communication with heaven, the paradoxical point of passage from one mode of being to another. We

shall soon see even clearer examples—sanctuaries that
are "doors of the gods" and hence places of passage
between heaven and earth.

Often there is no need for a theophany or hierophany
properly speaking; some *sign* suffices to indicate the
sacredness of a place. "According to the legend, the
marabout who founded El-Hamel at the end of the six-
teenth century stopped to spend the night near a spring
and planted his stick in the ground. The next morning,
when he went for it to resume his journey, he found that
it had taken root and that buds had sprouted on it. He
considered this a sign of God's will and settled in that
place."[1] In such cases the *sign*, fraught with religious
meaning, introduces an absolute element and puts an
end to relativity and confusion. *Something* that does not
belong to this world has manifested itself apodictically
and in so doing has indicated an orientation or determined a course of conduct.

When no sign manifests itself, it is *provoked*. For
example, a sort of *evocation* is performed with the help
of animals; it is they who *show* what place is fit to receive the sanctuary or the village. This amounts to an
evocation of sacred forms or figures for the immediate
purpose of establishing an *orientation* in the homogeneity of space. A *sign* is asked, to put an end to the
tension and anxiety caused by relativity and disorienta-

[1] René Basset, in *Revue des Traditions Populaires*, XXII, 1907, p. 287.

tion—in short, to reveal an absolute point of support.
For example, a wild animal is hunted, and the sanctuary
is built at the place where it is killed. Or a domestic
animal—such as a bull—is turned loose; some days
later it is searched for and sacrificed at the place where
it is found. Later the altar will be raised there and the
village will be built around the altar. In all these cases,
the sacrality of a place is revealed by animals. This is
as much as to say that men are not free to *choose* the
sacred site, that they only seek for it and find it by the
help of mysterious signs.

These few examples have shown the different means
by which religious man receives the revelation of a
sacred place. In each case the hierophany has annulled
the homogeneity of space and revealed a fixed point. But
since religious man cannot live except in an atmosphere
impregnated with the sacred, we must expect to find a
large number of techniques for consecrating space. As
we saw, the sacred is pre-eminently the *real*, at once
power, efficacity, the source of life and fecundity. Religious man's desire to live *in the sacred* is in fact equivalent to his desire to take up his abode in objective reality,
not to let himself be paralyzed by the never-ceasing
relativity of purely subjective experiences, to live in a
real and effective world, and not in an illusion. This
behavior is documented on every plane of religious
man's existence, but it is particularly evident in his
desire to move about only in a sanctified world, that is,

in a sacred space. This is the reason for the elaboration of techniques of *orientation* which, properly speaking, are techniques for the *construction* of sacred space. But we must not suppose that *human* work is in question here, that it is through his own efforts that man can consecrate a space. In reality the ritual by which he constructs a sacred space is efficacious in the measure in which *it reproduces the work of the gods*. But the better to understand the need for ritual construction of a sacred space, we must dwell a little on the traditional concept of the "world"; it will then be apparent that for religious man every world is a sacred world.

CHAOS AND COSMOS

One of the outstanding characteristics of traditional societies is the opposition that they assume between their inhabited territory and the unknown and indeterminate space that surrounds it. The former is the world (more precisely, *our* world), the cosmos; everything outside it is no longer a cosmos but a sort of "other world," a foreign, chaotic space, peopled by ghosts, demons, "foreigners" (who are assimilated to demons and the souls of the dead). At first sight this cleavage in space appears to be due to the opposition between an inhabited and organized—hence cosmicized —territory and the unknown space that extends beyond its frontiers; on one side there is a cosmos, on the other

a chaos. But we shall see that if every inhabited territory is a cosmos, this is precisely because it was first
consecrated, because, in one way or another, it is the
work of the gods or is in communication with the world
of the gods. The world (that is, our world) is a universe
within which the sacred has already manifested itself, in
which, consequently, the break-through from plane to
plane has become possible and repeatable. It is not
difficult to see why the religious moment implies the
cosmogonic moment. The sacred reveals absolute reality
and at the same time makes orientation possible; hence
it *founds the world* in the sense that it fixes the limits and
establishes the order of the world.

All this appears very clearly from the Vedic ritual for
taking possession of a territory; possession becomes
legally valid through the erection of a fire altar consecrated to Agni. "One says that one is installed when one
has built a fire altar [*gārhapatya*] and all those who
build the fire altar are legally established" (*Shatapatha
Brāhmana*, VII, 1, 1, 1-4). By the erection of a fire altar
Agni is made present, and communication with the
world of the gods is ensured; the space of the altar becomes a sacred space. But the meaning of the ritual is far
more complex, and if we consider all of its ramifications
we shall understand why consecrating a territory is
equivalent to making it a cosmos, to *cosmicizing* it. For,
in fact, the erection of an altar to Agni is nothing but the
reproduction—on the microcosmic scale—of the Creation. The water in which the clay is mixed is assimilated

to the primordial water; the clay that forms the base of the altar symbolizes the earth; the lateral walls represent the atmosphere, and so on. And the building of the altar is accompanied by songs that proclaim which cosmic region has just been created (*Shatapatha Brāhmana* I, 9, 2, 29, etc.). Hence the erection of a fire altar—which alone validates taking possession of a new territory—is equivalent to a cosmogony.

An unknown, foreign, and unoccupied territory (which often means, "unoccupied by our people") still shares in the fluid and larval modality of chaos. By occupying it and, above all, by settling in it, man symbolically transforms it into a cosmos through a ritual repetition of the cosmogony. What is to become "our world" must first be "created," and every creation has a paradigmatic model—the creation of the universe by the gods. When the Scandinavian colonists took possession of Iceland (*land-náma*) and cleared it, they regarded the enterprise neither as an original undertaking nor as human and profane work. For them, their labor was only repetition of a primordial act, the transformation of chaos into cosmos by the divine act of creation. When they tilled the desert soil, they were in fact repeating the act of the gods who had organized chaos by giving it a structure, forms, and norms.[2]

Whether it is a case of clearing uncultivated ground

[2] Cf. Mircea Eliade, *The Myth of the Eternal Return*, New York, Pantheon Books, Bollingen Series XLVI, 1954, pp. 11 ff. Cited hereafter as *Myth*.

or of conquering and occupying a territory already inhabited by "other" human beings, ritual taking possession must always repeat the cosmogony. For in the view of archaic societies everything that is not "our world" is not yet a world. A territory can be made ours only by creating it anew, that is, by consecrating it. This religious behavior in respect to unknown lands continued, even in the West, down to the dawn of modern times. The Spanish and Portuguese conquistadores, discovering and conquering territories, took possession of them in the name of Jesus Christ. The raising of the Cross was equivalent to consecrating the country, hence in some sort to a "new birth." For through Christ "old things are passed away; behold, all things are become new" (II Corinthians, 5, 17). The newly discovered country was "renewed," "re-created" by the Cross.

CONSECRATION OF A PLACE= REPETITION OF THE COSMOGONY

It must be understood that the cosmicization of unknown territories is always a consecration; to organize a space is to repeat the paradigmatic work of the gods. The close connection between cosmicization and consecration is already documented on the elementary levels of culture—for example, among the nomadic Australians whose economy is still at the stage of gathering and small-game hunting. According to the traditions of an

Arunta tribe, the Achilpa, in mythical times the divine being Numbakula cosmicized their future territory, created their Ancestor, and established their institutions. From the trunk of a gum tree Numbakula fashioned the sacred pole (*kauwa-auwa*) and, after anointing it with blood, climbed it and disappeared into the sky. This pole represents a cosmic axis, for it is around the sacred pole that territory becomes habitable, hence is transformed into a world. The sacred pole consequently plays an important role ritually. During their wanderings the Achilpa always carry it with them and choose the direction they are to take by the direction toward which it bends. This allows them, while being continually on the move, to be always in "their world" and, at the same time, in communication with the sky into which Numbakula vanished.

For the pole to be broken denotes catastrophe; it is like "the end of the world," reversion to chaos. Spencer and Gillen report that once, when the pole was broken, the entire clan were in consternation; they wandered about aimlessly for a time, and finally lay down on the ground together and waited for death to overtake them.[3]

This example admirably illustrates both the cosmological function of the sacred pole and its soteriological role. For on the one hand the *kauwa-auwa* reproduces the pole that Numbakula used to cosmicize the world,

[3] B. Spencer and F. J. Gillen, *The Arunta*, London, 1926, I, p. 388.

and on the other the Achilpa believe it to be the means by which they can communicate with the sky realm. Now, human existence is possible only by virtue of this permanent communication with the sky. The world of the Achilpa really becomes *their* world only in proportion as it reproduces the cosmos organized and sanctified by Numbakula. Life is not possible without an opening toward the transcendent; in other words, human beings cannot live in chaos. Once contact with the transcendent is lost, existence in the world ceases to be possible—and the Achilpa let themselves die.

To settle in a territory is, in the last analysis, equivalent to consecrating it. When settlement is not temporary, as among the nomads, but permanent, as among sedentary peoples, it implies a vital decision that involves the existence of the entire community. Establishment in a particular place, organizing it, inhabiting it, are acts that presuppose an existential choice—the choice of the universe that one is prepared to assume by "creating" it. Now, this universe is always the replica of the paradigmatic universe created and inhabited by the gods; hence it shares in the sanctity of the gods' work.

The sacred pole of the Achilpa supports *their* world and ensures communication with the sky. Here we have the prototype of a cosmological image that has been very widely disseminated—the cosmic pillars that support heaven and at the same time open the road to the world of the gods. Until their conversion to Christianity, the Celts and Germans still maintained their worship of such sacred pillars. The *Chronicum Laurissense breve,* written about 800, reports that in the course of one of his wars against the Saxons (772), Charlemagne destroyed the temple and the sacred wood of their "famous Irminsul" in the town of Eresburg. Rudolf of Fulda (*c.* 860) adds that this famous pillar is the "pillar of the universe which, as it were, supports all things" (*universalis columna quasi sustinens omnia*). The same cosmological image is found not only among the Romans (Horace, *Odes,* III, 3) and in ancient India, where we hear of the *skambha,* the cosmic pillar (*Rig Veda,* I, 105; X, 89, 4; etc.), but also among the Canary Islanders and in such distant cultures as those of the Kwakiutl (British Columbia) and of the Nad'a of Flores Island (Indonesia). The Kwakiutl believe that a copper pole passes through the three cosmic levels (underworld, earth, sky); the point at which it enters the sky is the "door to the world above." The visible image of this cosmic pillar in the sky is the Milky Way. But the work of the gods, the universe, is repeated and imitated by men on their own scale. The *axis mundi,* seen in the sky in the form of the Milky Way, appears in the ceremonial house in the form of a sacred pole. It is the trunk of a cedar tree, thirty to thirty-five feet high, over half of which projects through the roof. This pillar plays a primary part in the ceremonies; it confers a cosmic structure on the house. In the ritual songs the house is called "our world" and the candidates for initiation, who live in it, proclaim: "I am at the Center of the World. . . . I am at the Post of the World," and so on.[4] The same assimilation of the cosmic pillar to the sacred pole and of the ceremonial house to the universe is found among the Nad'a of Flores Island. The sacrificial pole is called the "Pole of Heaven" and is believed to support the sky.[5]

THE CENTER OF THE WORLD

The cry of the Kwakiutl neophyte, "I am at the Center of the World!" at once reveals one of the deepest meanings of sacred space. Where the break-through from plane to plane has been effected by a hierophany, there too an opening has been made, either upward (the divine world) or downward (the underworld, the world of the dead). The three cosmic levels—earth, heaven, underworld—have been put in communication. As we just saw, this communication is sometimes expressed through the image of a universal pillar, *axis mundi,* which at once connects and supports heaven and earth and whose base is fixed in the world below (the infernal

[4] Werner Müller, *Weltbild und Kult der Kwakiutl-Indianer,* Wiesbaden, 1955, pp. 17-20.
[5] P. Arndt, "Die Megalithenkultur des Nad'a" (*Anthropos* 27, 1932), pp 61-62.

regions). Such a cosmic pillar can be only at the very center of the universe, for the whole of the habitable world extends around it. Here, then, we have a sequence of religious conceptions and cosmological images that are inseparably connected and form a system that may be called the "system of the world" prevalent in traditional societies: (*a*) a sacred place constitutes a break in the homogeneity of space; (*b*) this break is symbolized by an opening by which passage from one cosmic region to another is made possible (from heaven to earth and vice versa; from earth to the underworld); (*c*) communication with heaven is expressed by one or another of certain images, all of which refer to the *axis mundi*: pillar (cf. the *universalis columna*), ladder (cf. Jacob's ladder), mountain, tree, vine, etc.; (*d*) around this cosmic axis lies the world (= our world), hence the axis is located "in the middle," at the "navel of the earth"; it is the Center of the World.

Many different myths, rites, and beliefs are derived from this traditional "system of the world." They cannot all be mentioned here. Rather, we shall confine ourselves to a few examples, taken from various civilizations and particularly suited to demonstrate the role of sacred space in the life of traditional societies. Whether that space appears in the form of a sacred precinct, a ceremonial house, a city, a world, we everywhere find the symbolism of the Center of the World; and it is this symbolism which, in the majority of cases, explains re-

ligious behavior in respect to the space in which one
lives.

We shall begin with an example that has the advantage of immediately showing not only the consistency
but also the complexity of this type of symbolism—the
cosmic mountain. We have just seen that the mountain
occurs among the images that express the connection
between heaven and earth; hence it is believed to be at
the center of the world. And in a number of cultures we
do in fact hear of such mountains, real or mythical, situated at the center of the world; examples are Meru in
India, Haraberezaiti in Iran, the mythical "Mount of the
Lands" in Mesopotamia, Gerizim in Palestine—which,
moreover, was called the "navel of the earth."[6] Since the
sacred mountain is an *axis mundi* connecting earth with
heaven, it in a sense touches heaven and hence marks
the highest point in the world; consequently the territory
that surrounds it, and that constitutes "our world," is
held to be the highest among countries. This is stated in
Hebrew tradition: Palestine, being the highest land, was
not submerged by the Flood.[7] According to Islamic tradition, the highest place on earth is the *kā'aba,* because
"the Pole Star bears witness that it faces the center of
Heaven."[8] For Christians, it is Golgotha that is on the
summit of the cosmic mountain. All these beliefs express

[6] See the bibliographical references in Eliade, *Myth*, pp. 10 ff.
[7] A. E. Wensinck and E. Burrows, cited in *ibid.*, p. 10.
[8] Wensinck, cited in *ibid.*, p. 15.

the same feeling, which is profoundly religious: "our world" is holy ground *because it is the place nearest to heaven,* because from here, from our abode, it is possible to reach heaven; hence our world is a high place. In cosmological terms, this religious conception is expressed by the projection of the favored territory which is "ours" onto the summit of the cosmic mountain. Later speculation drew all sorts of conclusions—for example, the one just cited for Palestine, that the Holy Land was not submerged by the Flood.

This same symbolism of the center explains other series of cosmological images and religious beliefs. Among these the most important are: (*a*) holy sites and sanctuaries are believed to be situated at the center of the world; (*b*) temples are replicas of the cosmic mountain and hence constitute the pre-eminent "link" between earth and heaven; (*c*) the foundations of temples descend deep into the lower regions. A few examples will suffice. After citing them, we shall attempt to integrate all these various aspects of the same symbolism; the remarkable consistency of these traditional conceptions of the world will then appear with greater clarity.

The capital of the perfect Chinese sovereign is located at the center of the world; there, on the day of the summer solstice, the gnomon must cast no shadow.[9] It is striking that the same symbolism is found in regard to

[9] M. Granet, in Eliade, *Patterns,* p. 376.

the Temple of Jerusalem; the rock on which it was built was the navel of the earth. The Icelandic pilgrim, Nicholas of Thverva, who visited Jerusalem in the twelfth century, wrote of the Holy Sepulcher: "The Center of the World is there; there, on the day of the summer solstice, the light of the Sun falls perpendicularly from Heaven."[10] The same conception occurs in Iran; the Iranian land (*Airyanam Vaejah*) is the center and heart of the world. Just as the heart lies at the center of the body, "the land of Iran is more precious than all other countries because it is set at the middle of the world."[11] This is why Shiz, the "Jerusalem" of the Iranians (for it lay at the center of the world) was held to be the original site of the royal power and, at the same time, the birthplace of Zarathustra.[12]

As for the assimilation of temples to cosmic mountains and their function as links between earth and heaven, the names given to Babylonian sanctuaries themselves bear witness; they are called "Mountain of the House," "House of the Mountain of all Lands," "Mountain of Storms," "Link between Heaven and Earth," and the like. The ziggurat was literally a cosmic mountain; the seven stories represented the seven planetary heavens; by ascending them, the priest reached the summit of the

[10] L. I. Ringbom, *Graltempel und Paradies*, Stockholm, 1951, p. 255.
[11] *Sad-dar*, 84, 4-5, cited in Ringbom, p. 327.
[12] See the material assembled and discussed in Ringbom, pp. 294 ff. and *passim*.

universe. A like symbolism explains the immense temple of Borobudur, in Java; it is built as an artificial mountain. Ascending it is equivalent to an ecstatic journey to the center of the world; reaching the highest terrace, the pilgrim experiences a break-through from plane to plane; he enters a "pure region" transcending the profane world.

Dur-an-ki, "Link between Heaven and Earth," was a name applied to a number of Babylonian sanctuaries (it occurs at Nippur, Larsa, Sippara, and elsewhere). Babylon had many names, among them "House of the Base of Heaven and Earth," "Link between Heaven and Earth." But it was also in Babylon that the connection between earth and the lower regions was made, for the city had been built on *bāb apsī*, "the Gate of Apsū," *apsū* being the name for the waters of chaos before Creation. The same tradition is found among the Hebrews; the rock of the Temple in Jerusalem reached deep into the *tehōm*, the Hebrew equivalent of *apsū*. And, just as Babylon had its Gate of Apsū, the rock of the temple in Jerusalem contained the "mouth of the *tehōm*."[13]

The *apsū*, the *tehōm* symbolize the chaos of waters, *the preformal modality of cosmic matter*, and, at the same time, the world of death, of all that precedes and follows life. The Gate of Apsū and the rock containing the "mouth of the *tehōm*" designate not only the point of

[13] Cf. the references in Eliade, *Myth*, pp. 15 ff.

intersection—and hence of communication—between the lower world and earth, but also *the difference in onto-logical status between these two cosmic planes.* There is a break of plane between the *tehōm* and the rock of the Temple that blocks its mouth, passage from the virtual to the formal, from death to life. The watery chaos that preceded Creation at the same time symbolizes the retro-gression to the formless that follows on death, return to the larval modality of existence. From one point of view, the lower regions can be homologized to the unknown and desert regions that surround the inhabited territory; the underworld, over which our cosmos is firmly estab-lished, corresponds to the chaos that extends to its frontiers.

"OUR WORLD" IS ALWAYS SITUATED AT THE CENTER

From all that has been said, it follows that the true world is always in the middle, at the Center, for it is here that there is a break in plane and hence com-munication among the three cosmic zones. Whatever the extent of the territory involved, the cosmos that it repre-sents is always perfect. An entire country (*e.g.,* Pales-tine), a city (Jerusalem), a sanctuary (the Temple in Jerusalem), all equally well present an *imago mundi.* Treating of the symbolism of the Temple, Flavius Jose-phus wrote that the court represented the sea (*i.e.,* the lower regions), the Holy Place represented earth, and the Holy of Holies heaven (*Ant. Jud.*, III, 7, 7). It is clear, then, that both the *imago mundi* and the Center are repeated in the inhabited world. Palestine, Jerusalem, and the Temple severally and concurrently represent the image of the universe and the Center of the World. This multiplicity of centers and this reiteration of the image of the world on smaller and smaller scales constitute one of the specific characteristics of traditional societies.

To us, it seems an inescapable conclusion that *the religious man sought to live as near as possible to the Center of the World.* He knew that his country lay at the midpoint of the earth; he knew too that his city constituted the navel of the universe, and, above all, that the temple or the palace were veritably Centers of the World. But he also wanted his own house to be at the Center and to be an *imago mundi*. And, in fact, as we shall see, houses are held to be at the Center of the World and, on the microcosmic scale, to reproduce the universe. In other words, the man of traditional societies could only live in a space opening upward, where the break in plane was symbolically assured and hence communication with the *other world*, the transcendental world, was ritually possible. Of course the sanctuary—the Center par excellence—was there, close to him, in the city, and he could be sure of communicating with the world of the gods simply by entering the temple. But he felt the need to live at the Center *always*—like the Achilpa, who, as we saw, always carried the sacred pole, the *axis mundi*, with them, so that they should never be far from the Center and should remain in communication with the supraterrestrial world. In short, whatever the dimensions of the space with which he is familiar and in which he regards himself as situated—his country, his city, his village, his house—religious man feels the need always to exist in a total and organized world, in a cosmos.

A universe comes to birth from its center; it spreads out from a central point that is, as it were, its navel. It is in this way that, according to the *Rig Veda* (X, 149), the universe was born and developed—from a core, a central point. Hebrew tradition is still more explicit: "The Most Holy One created the world like an embryo. As the embryo grows from the navel, so God began to create the world by the navel and from there it spread out in all directions." And since the "navel of the earth," the Center of the World, is the Holy Land, the *Yoma* affirms that "the world was created beginning with Zion."[14] Rabbi ben Gorion said of the rock of Jerusalem: "it is called the Foundation Stone of the Earth, that is, the navel of the Earth, because it is from there that the whole Earth unfolded."[15] Then too, because the creation of man is a replica of the cosmogony, it follows that the first man was fashioned at the "navel of the earth" or in

[14] References in *ibid.*, p. 16.
[15] Cited in W. W. Roscher, "Neue Omphalosstudien" (*Abh. der Königl. Sächs. Ges. d. Wiss., Phil.-hist. Klasse*, 31, 1, 1915), p. 16.

Jerusalem (Judaeo-Christian traditions). It could not be otherwise, if we remember that the Center is precisely the place where a break in plane occurs, where space becomes sacred, hence pre-eminently *real*. A creation implies a superabundance of reality, in other words an irruption of the sacred into the world.

It follows that *every construction or fabrication has the cosmogony as paradigmatic model*. The creation of the world becomes the archetype of every creative human gesture, whatever its plane of reference may be. We have already seen that settling in a territory reiterates the cosmogony. Now that the cosmogonic value of the Center has become clear, we can still better understand why every human establishment repeats the creation of the world from a central point (the navel). Just as the universe unfolds from a center and stretches out toward the four cardinal points, the village comes into existence around an intersection. In Bali, as in some parts of Asia, when a new village is to be built the people look for a natural intersection, where two roads cross at right angles. A square constructed from a central point is an *imago mundi*. The division of the village into four sections—which incidentally implies a similar division of the community—corresponds to the division of the universe into four horizons. A space is often left empty in the middle of the village; there the ceremonial house will later be built, with its roof symbolically representing heaven (in some cases, heaven is indicated by the top of a tree or by the image of a mountain). At the other end of the same perpendicular axis lies the world of the dead, symbolized by certain animals (snake, crocodile, etc.) or by ideograms expressing darkness.[16]

The cosmic symbolism of the village is repeated in the structure of the sanctuary or the ceremonial house. At Waropen, in New Guinea, the "men's house" stands at the center of the village; its roof represents the celestial vault, the four walls correspond to the four directions of space. In Ceram, the sacred stone of the village symbolizes heaven and the four stone columns that support it incarnate the four pillars that support heaven.[17] Similar conceptions are found among the Algonquins and the Sioux. Their sacred lodge, where initiations are performed, represents the universe. The roof symbolizes the dome of the sky, the floor represents earth, the four walls the four directions of cosmic space. The ritual construction of the space is emphasized by a threefold symbolism: the four doors, the four windows, and the four colors signify the four cardinal points. The construction of the sacred lodge thus repeats the cosmogony, for the lodge represents the world.[18]

We are not surprised to find a similar concept in an-

[16] Cf. C. T. Bertling, *Vierzahl, Kreuz und Mandala in Asien*, Amsterdam, 1954, pp. 8 ff.

[17] See the references in Bertling, *op. cit.*, pp. 4-5.

[18] See the material and interpretations in Werner Müller, *Die blaue Hütte*, Wiesbaden, 1954, pp. 60 ff.

cient Italy and among the ancient Germans. In short, the underlying idea is both archaic and widely disseminated: from a center, the four horizons are projected in the four cardinal directions. The Roman *mundus* was a circular trench divided into four parts; it was at once the image of the cosmos and the paradigmatic model for the human habitation. It has been rightly proposed that *Roma quadrata* is to be understood not as being square in shape but as being divided into four parts.[19] The *mundus* was clearly assimilated to the *omphalos*, to the navel of the earth; the city (*urbs*) was situated in the middle of the *orbis terrarum*. Similar ideas have been shown to explain the structure of Germanic villages and towns.[20] In extremely varied cultural contexts, we constantly find the same cosmological schema and the same ritual scenario: *settling in a territory is equivalent to founding a world.*

CITY-COSMOS

Since "our world" is a cosmos, any attack from without threatens to turn it into chaos. And as "our world" was founded by imitating the paradigmatic work of the gods, the cosmogony, so the enemies who attack it are assimilated to the enemies of the gods, the demons, and especially to the archdemon, the primordial dragon

19 F. Altheim, in Werner Müller, *Kreis und Kreuz*, Berlin, 1938, pp. 60 ff.
20 W. Müller, *op. cit.*, pp. 65 ff.

conquered by the gods at the beginning of time. An attack on "our world" is equivalent to an act of revenge by the mythical dragon, who rebels against the work of the gods, the cosmos, and struggles to annihilate it. "Our" enemies belong to the powers of chaos. *Any destruction of a city is equivalent to a retrogression to chaos. Any victory over the attackers reiterates the paradigmatic victory of the gods over the dragon (that is, over chaos).*

This is the reason the Pharaoh was assimilated to the God Rē, conqueror of the dragon Apophis, while his enemies were assimilated to the mythical dragon. Darius regarded himself as a new Thraetaona, the mythical Iranian hero who was said to have slain a three-headed dragon. In Judaic tradition the pagan kings were represented in the likeness of the dragon; such is the Nebuchadnezzar described by Jeremiah (51, 34) and the Pompey presented in the Psalms of Solomon (9, 29).

As we shall see later, the dragon is the paradigmatic figure of the marine monster, of the primordial snake, symbol of the cosmic waters, of darkness, night, and death—in short, of the amorphous and virtual, of everything that has not yet acquired a "form." The dragon must be conquered and cut to pieces by the gods so that the cosmos may come to birth. It was from the body of the marine monster Tiamat that Marduk fashioned the world. Yahweh created the universe after his victory over the primordial monster Rahab. But, as we shall see, this victory of the gods over the dragon must be symbolically repeated each year, for each year the world must be created anew. Similarly the victory of the gods over the forces of darkness, death, and chaos is repeated with every victory of the city over its invaders.

It is highly probable that the fortifications of inhabited places and cities began by being magical defenses; for fortifications—trenches, labyrinths, ramparts, etc.— were designed rather to repel invasion by demons and the souls of the dead than attacks by human beings. In North India, during epidemics, a circle is drawn around the village to keep the demons of sickness from entering the enclosure.[21] In Europe, during the Middle Ages, the walls of cities were ritually consecrated as a defense against the devil, sickness, and death. Then, too, symbolic thinking finds no difficulty in assimilating the human enemy to the devil and death. In the last analysis the result of attacks, whether demonic or military, is always the same—ruin, disintegration, death.

It is worth observing that the same images are still used in our own day to formulate the dangers that threaten a certain type of civilization; we speak of the chaos, the disorder, the darkness that will overwhelm "our world." All these terms express the abolition of an order, a cosmos, an organic structure, and reimmersion in the state of fluidity, of formlessness—in short, of

[21] Eliade, *Patterns,* p. 371.

chaos. This, in our opinion, shows that the paradigmatic images live on in the language and clichés of nonreligious man. Something of the religious conception of the world still persists in the behavior of profane man, although he is not always conscious of this immemorial heritage.

UNDERTAKING THE CREATION OF THE WORLD

Let us consider the basic difference observable between these two types of behavior—traditional religious and profane—in respect to the human habitation. There is no need to dwell on the value and function of the habitation in industrial societies; they are well known. According to the formula of a famous contemporary architect, Le Corbusier, the house is "a machine to live in." Hence it takes its place among the countless machines mass-produced in industrial societies. The ideal house of the modern world must first of all be functional; that is, it must allow men to work and to rest in order that they may work. You can change your "machine to live in" as often as you change your bicycle, your refrigerator, your automobile. You can also change cities or provinces, without encountering any difficulties aside from those that arise from a difference in climate.

It does not lie within our province to write the history of the gradual desacralization of the human dwelling.

The process is an integral part of the gigantic transformation of the world undertaken by the industrial societies, a transformation made possible by the desacralization of the cosmos accomplished by scientific thought and above all by the sensational discoveries of physics and chemistry. We shall later have occasion to inquire whether this secularization of nature is really final, if no possibility remains for nonreligious man to rediscover the sacred dimension of existence in the world. As we just saw, and as we shall see still more clearly later, certain traditional images, certain vestiges of the behavior of archaic man still persist, in the condition of "survivals," even in the most highly industrialized societies. But for the moment our concern is to describe, in its pure state, religious behavior in respect to the habitation, and to discover the *Weltanschauung* that it implies.

As we saw, to settle in a territory, to build a dwelling, demand a vital decision for both the whole community and the individual. For what is involved is *undertaking the creation of the world that one has chosen to inhabit.* Hence it is necessary to imitate the work of the gods, the cosmogony. But this is not always easy, for there are also tragic, blood-drenched cosmogonies; as imitator of the divine gestures, man must reiterate them. Since the gods had to slay and dismember a marine monster or a primordial being in order to create the world from it, man in his turn must imitate them when he builds his own world, his city or his house. Hence the necessity for

bloody or symbolic sacrifices on the occasion of constructions, the countless forms of the *Bauopfer* (building sacrifice), concerning which we shall have to say a
few words further on.

Whatever the structure of a traditional society—be it
a society of hunters, herdsmen, or cultivators, or already
at the stage of urban civilization—the habitation always
undergoes a process of sanctification, because it constitutes an *imago mundi* and the world is a divine creation.
But there are various ways of homologizing the dwelling place to the cosmos, because there are various types
of cosmogonies. For our purpose, it will suffice to distinguish two methods of ritually transforming the dwelling place (whether the territory or the house) into cosmos, that is, of giving it the value of an *imago mundi*:
(*a*) assimilating it to the cosmos by the projection of the
four horizons from a central point (in the case of a
village) or by the symbolic installation of the *axis mundi*
(in the case of a house); (*b*) repeating, through a ritual
of construction, the paradigmatic acts of the gods by
virtue of which the world came to birth from the body of
a marine dragon or of a primordial giant. We need not
here dwell on the basic differences in *Weltanschauung*
underlying these two methods of sanctifying the dwelling place, nor on their historical and cultural presuppositions. Suffice it to say that the first method—
cosmicizing a space by projection of the horizons or by
installation of the *axis mundi*—is already documented

in the most archaic stages of culture (cf. the *kauwa-auwa* pole of the Australian Achilpa), while the second method seems to have been developed in the culture of the earliest cultivators. What is important for our investigation is the fact that, in all traditional cultures, the habitation possesses a sacred aspect by the simple fact that it reflects the world.

Thus, in the habitation of the primitive peoples of the North American and North Asian Arctics we find a central post that is assimilated to the *axis mundi*, *i.e.*, to the cosmic pillar or the world tree, which, as we saw, connect earth with heaven. In other words, *cosmic symbolism is found in the very structure of the habitation*. The house is an *imago mundi*. The sky is conceived as a vast tent supported by a central pillar; the tent pole or the central post of the house is assimilated to the Pillars of the World and is so named. This central pole or post has an important ritual role; the sacrifices in honor of the celestial Supreme Being are performed at the foot of it. The same symbolism has been preserved among the herdsmen-breeders of Central Asia, but since here the conical-roofed habitation with central pillar is replaced by the yurt, the mythico-ritual function of the pillar is transferred to the upper opening for the escape of smoke. Like the pole (= *axis mundi*), the stripped tree trunk whose top emerges through the upper opening of the yurt (and which symbolizes the cosmic tree) is conceived as a ladder leading to heaven; the shamans climb it on their celestial journeys. And it is through the upper opening that the shamans set out on their flights.[22] The sacred pillar, set in the middle of the habitation, is found again in Africa among the Hamitic and Hamitoid pastoral peoples.[23]

COSMOGONY AND BUILDING SACRIFICE

A similar conception is found in such a highly evolved culture as that of India; but here there is also an exemplification of the other method of homologizing the house to the cosmos, to which we referred briefly above. Before the masons lay the first stone the astronomer shows them the spot where it is to be placed, and this spot is supposed to lie above the snake that supports the world. The master mason sharpens a stake and drives it into the ground, exactly at the indicated spot, in order to fix the snake's head. A foundation stone is then laid above the stake. *Thus the cornerstone is at the exact center of the world.*[24] But, in addition, the act of foundation repeats the cosmogonic act; for to drive the stake into the snake's head to "fix" it is to imitate the primordial gesture of Soma or Indra, when the latter, as the *Rig Veda* expresses it, "struck the Snake in his lair" (IV, 17,

---

[22] M. Eliade, *Le Chamanisme et les techniques archaïques de l'extase*, Paris, 1951, pp. 238 ff. Cited hereafter as *Le Chamanisme*.

[23] Wilhelm Schmidt, "Der heilige Mittelpfahl des Hauses," *Anthropos*, 35-36, 1940-1941, p. 967.

[24] S. Stevenson, *The Rites of the Twice-Born*, Oxford, 1920, p. 354.

9), when his lightning bolt "cut off its head" (I, 52, 10). As we said, *the snake symbolizes chaos, the formless, the unmanifested. To behead it is equivalent to an act of creation, passage from the virtual and the amorphous to that which has form.* Again, it was from the body of a primordial marine monster, Tiamat, that the god Marduk fashioned the world. This victory was symbolically repeated each year, since each year the cosmos was renewed. But the paradigmatic act of the divine victory was likewise repeated on the occasion of every construction, for every new construction reproduced the creation of the world.

This second type of cosmogony is much more complex, and it will only be outlined here. But it was necessary to cite it, for, in the last analysis, it is with such a cosmogony that the countless forms of the building sacrifice are bound up; the latter, in short, is only an imitation, often a symbolic imitation, of the primordial sacrifice that gave birth to the world. For, beginning with a certain stage of culture, the cosmogonic myth explains the Creation through the slaying of a giant (Ymir in Germanic mythology, Purusha in Indian mythology, P'an-ku in China); his organs give birth to the various cosmic regions. According to other groups of myths, it is not only the cosmos that comes to birth in consequence of the immolation of a primordial being and from his own substance, but also food plants, the races of man, or different social classes. It is on this type of cosmogonic myth that building sacrifices depend. If a "construction" is to endure (be it house, temple, tool, etc.), it must be animated, that is, it must receive life and a soul. The transfer of the soul is possible only through a blood sacrifice. The history of religions, ethnology, folklore record countless forms of building sacrifices—that is, of symbolic or blood sacrifices for the benefit of a structure.[25] In southeastern Europe, these beliefs have inspired admirable popular ballads describing the sacrifice of the wife of the master mason in order that a structure may be completed (cf. the ballads on the Arta Bridge in Greece, on the Monastery of Argesh in Romania, on the city of Scutari in Yugoslavia, etc.).

We have said enough about the religious significance of the human dwelling place for certain conclusions to have become self-evident. Exactly like the city or the sanctuary, the house is sanctified, in whole or part, by a cosmological symbolism or ritual. This is why settling somewhere—building a village or merely a house—represents a serious decision, for the very existence of man is involved; he must, in short, create his own world and assume the responsibility of maintaining and renewing it. Habitations are not lightly changed, for it is not easy to abandon one's world. The house is not an object, a "machine to live in"; *it is the universe that man constructs for himself by imitating the paradigmatic crea-*

[25] Cf. Paul Sartori, "Über das Bauopfer," *Zeitschrift für Ethnologie*, 30, 1938, pp. 1-54.

tion of the gods, the cosmogony. Every construction and every inauguration of a new dwelling are in some measure equivalent to a *new beginning,* a *new life.* And every beginning repeats the primordial beginning, when the universe first saw the light of day. Even in modern societies, with their high degree of desacralization, the festivity and rejoicing that accompany settling in a new house still preserve the memory of the festival exuberance that, long ago, marked the *incipit vita nova.*

Since the habitation constitutes an *imago mundi,* it is symbolically situated at the Center of the World. The multiplicity, or even the infinity, of centers of the world raises no difficulty for religious thought. For it is not a matter of geometrical space, but of an existential and sacred space that has an entirely different structure, that admits of an infinite number of breaks and hence is capable of an infinite number of communications with the transcendent. We have seen the cosmological meaning and the ritual role of the upper opening in various forms of habitations. In other cultures these cosmological meanings and ritual functions are transferred to the chimney (= smoke hole) and to the part of the roof that lies above the "sacred area" and that is removed or even broken in cases of prolonged death-agony. When we come to the homologation cosmos-house-human body, we shall have occasion to show the deeper meaning of "breaking the roof." For the moment, we will mention that the most ancient sanctuaries were hypaethral or built with an aperture in the roof—the "eye of the dome," symbolizing break-through from plane to plane, communication with the transcendent.

Thus *religious architecture simply took over and developed the cosmological symbolism already present in the structure of primitive habitations.* In its turn, the human habitation had been chronologically preceded by the provisional "holy place," by a space provisionally consecrated and cosmicized (cf. the Australian Achilpa). This is as much as to say that all symbols and rituals having to do with temples, cities, and houses *are finally derived from the primary experience of sacred space.*

TEMPLE, BASILICA, CATHEDRAL

In the great oriental civilizations—from Mesopotamia and Egypt to China and India—the temple received a new and important valorization. It is not only an *imago mundi*; it is also interpreted as the earthly reproduction of a transcendent model. Judaism inherited this ancient oriental conception of the temple as the copy of a celestial work of architecture. In this idea we probably have one of the last interpretations that religious man has given to the primary experience of sacred space in contrast to profane space. Hence we must dwell a little on the perspectives opened by this new religious conception.

To summarize the essential data of the problem: If

the temple constitutes an *imago mundi,* this is because
the world, as the work of the gods, is sacred. But the
cosmological structure of the temple gives room for a
new religious valorization; as house of the gods, hence
holy place above all others, the temple continually
resanctifies the world, because it at once represents and
contains it. In the last analysis, *it is by virtue of the
temple that the world is resanctified in every part.* However impure it may have become, the world is continually
purified by the sanctity of sanctuaries.

Another idea derives from this increasingly accepted
ontological difference between the *cosmos* and *its sanctified image,* the temple. This is the idea that the sanctity
of the temple is proof against all earthly corruption, by
virtue of the fact that the architectural plan of the temple
is the work of the gods and hence exists in heaven, near
to the gods. The transcendent models of temples enjoy a
spiritual, incorruptible celestial existence. Through the
grace of the gods, man attains to the dazzling vision of
these models, which he then attempts to reproduce on
earth. The Babylonian king Gudea saw in a dream the
goddess Nidaba showing him a tablet on which were
written the names of the beneficent stars, and a god revealed the plan of the temple to him.[26] Sennacherib built
Nineveh according to "the plan established from most
distant times in the configuration of the Heavens." This

[26] Cf. Eliade, *Myth,* pp. 7-8.

means not only that celestial geometry made the first constructions possible, but above all that since the architectonic models were in heaven, they shared in the sacrality of the sky.

For the people of Israel, the models of the tabernacle, of all the sacred utensils, and of the temple itself had been created by Yahweh who revealed them to his chosen, to be reproduced on earth. Thus Yahweh says to Moses: "And let them make me a sanctuary; that I may dwell among them. According to all that I shew thee, after the pattern of the tabernacle, and the pattern of all the instruments thereof, even so shall ye make it" (Exodus, 25, 8-9). "And look that thou make them after their pattern, which was shewed thee in the mount" (*ibid.*, 25, 40). When David gives his son Solomon the plans for the Temple buildings, the tabernacle, and all the utensils, he assures him that "all this . . . the Lord made me understand in writing by his hand upon me" (II Chronicles, 28, 19). He must, then, have seen the celestial model created by Yahweh from the beginning of time. This is what Solomon affirms: "Thou hast commanded me to build a temple upon thy holy mount, and an altar in the city wherein thou dwellest, a resemblance of the holy tabernacle which thou hast prepared from the beginning" (Wisdom of Solomon, 9, 8).

The Heavenly Jerusalem was created by God at the same time as Paradise, hence *in aeternum.* The city of Jerusalem was only an approximate reproduction of the transcendent model; it could be polluted by man, but the model was incorruptible, for it was not involved in time. "This building now built in your midst is not that which is revealed with Me, that which was prepared beforehand here from the time when I took counsel to make Paradise, and showed it to Adam before he sinned" (II Baruch, 4, 3-7; trans. R. H. Charles[27]).

The Christian basilica and, later, the cathedral take over and continue all these symbolisms. On the one hand, the church is conceived as imitating the Heavenly Jerusalem, even from patristic times; on the other, it also reproduces Paradise or the celestial world. But the cosmological structure of the sacred edifice still persists in the thought of Christendom; for example, it is obvious in the Byzantine church. "The four parts of the interior of the church symbolize the four cardinal directions. The interior of the church is the universe. The altar is paradise, which lay in the East. The imperial door to the altar was also called the Door of Paradise. During Easter week, the great door to the altar remains open during the entire service; the meaning of this custom is clearly expressed in the Easter Canon: 'Christ rose from the grave and opened the doors of Paradise unto us.' The West, on the contrary, is the realm of darkness, of grief, of death, the realm of the eternal mansions of the dead, who await the resurrection of the flesh and the

[27] R. H. Charles, ed., *The Apocrypha and Pseudepigrapha of the Old Testament in English*, Oxford, 1913, Vol. II, p. 482.

Last Judgment. The middle of the building is the earth. According to the views of Kosmas Indikopleustes, the earth is rectangular and is bounded by four walls, which are surmounted by a dome. The four parts of the interior of the church symbolize the four cardinal directions."[28] As "copy of the cosmos," the Byzantine church incarnates and at the same time sanctifies the world.

SOME CONCLUSIONS

From the thousands of examples available to the historian of religions, we have cited only a small number but enough to show the varieties of the religious experience of space. We have taken our examples from different cultures and periods, in order to present at least the most important mythological constructions and ritual scenarios that are based on the experience of sacred space. For in the course of history, religious man has given differing valorizations to the same fundamental experience. We need only compare the conception of the sacred space (and hence of the cosmos) discernible among the Australian Achilpa with the corresponding conceptions of the Kwakiutl, the Altaic peoples, or the Mesopotamians, to realize the differences among them. There is no need to dwell on the truism that, since the religious life of humanity is realized in history, its expressions are inevitably conditioned by the variety of

[28] Hans Sedlmayr, *Die Entstehung der Kathedrale*, Zurich, 1950, p. 119.

historical moments and cultural styles. But for our purpose it is not the infinite variety of the religious experiences of space that concerns us but, on the contrary, their elements of unity. Pointing out the contrast between the behavior of nonreligious man with respect to the space in which he lives and the behavior of religious man in respect to sacred space is enough to make the difference in structure between the two attitudes clearly apparent.

If we should attempt to summarize the result of the descriptions that have been presented in this chapter, we could say that the experience of sacred space makes possible the "founding of the world": where the sacred manifests itself in space, *the real unveils itself*, the world comes into existence. But the irruption of the sacred does not only project a fixed point into the formless fluidity of profane space, a center into chaos; it also effects a break in plane, that is, it opens communication between the cosmic planes (between earth and heaven) and makes possible ontological passage from one mode of being to another. It is such a break in the heterogeneity of profane space that creates the center through which communication with the transmundane is established, that, consequently, founds the world, for the center renders *orientation* possible. Hence the manifestation of the sacred in space has a cosmological valence; every spatial hierophany or consecration of a space is equivalent to a cosmogony. The first conclusion we might draw would be: *the world becomes apprehensible as world, as cosmos, in the measure in which it reveals itself as a sacred world.*

Every world is the work of the gods, for it was either created directly by the gods or was consecrated, hence cosmicized, by men ritually reactualizing the paradigmatic act of Creation. This is as much as to say that religious man can live only in a sacred world, because it is only in such a world that he participates in being, that he has a *real existence.* This religious need expresses an unquenchable ontological thirst. Religious man thirsts for *being.* His terror of the chaos that surrounds his inhabited world corresponds to his terror of nothingness. The unknown space that extends beyond his world—an uncosmicized because unconsecrated space, a mere amorphous extent into which no orientation has yet been projected, and hence in which no structure has yet arisen —for religious man, this profane space represents absolute nonbeing. If, by some evil chance, he strays into it, he feels emptied of his ontic substance, as if he were dissolving in Chaos, and he finally dies.

This ontological thirst is manifested in many ways. In the realm of sacred space which we are now considering, its most striking manifestation is religious man's will to take his stand at the very heart of the real, at the Center of the World—that is, exactly where the cosmos came into existence and began to spread out toward the four horizons, and where, too, there is the possibility of communication with the gods; in short, precisely where

he is *closest to the gods.* We have seen that the symbolism of the center is the formative principle not only of
countries, cities, temples, and palaces but also of the
humblest human dwelling, be it the tent of a nomad
hunter, the shepherd's yurt, or the house of the sedentary
cultivator. This is as much as to say that every religious
man places himself at the Center of the World and by
the same token at the very source of absolute reality, as
close as possible to the opening that ensures him communication with the gods.

But since to settle somewhere, to inhabit a space, is
equivalent to repeating the cosmogony and hence to imitating the work of the gods, it follows that, for religious
man, every existential decision to situate himself in space
in fact constitutes a religious decision. By assuming the
responsibility of creating the world that he has chosen
to inhabit, he not only cosmicizes chaos but also sanctifies his little cosmos by making it like the world of the
gods. Religious man's profound nostalgia is to inhabit
a "divine world," is his desire that his house shall be
like the house of the gods, as it was later represented in
temples and sanctuaries. In short, this religious nostalgia
expresses *the desire to live in a pure and holy cosmos,
as it was in the beginning, when it came fresh from the
Creator's hands.*

The experience of sacred time will make it possible
for religious man periodically to experience the cosmos
as it was *in principio,* that is, at the mythical moment of
Creation.

CHAPTER 2

Sacred Time

and Myths

PROFANE DURATION AND SACRED TIME

For religious man time too, like space, is neither homogeneous nor continuous. On the one hand there are the intervals of a sacred time, the time of festivals (by far the greater part of which are periodical); on the other there is profane time, ordinary temporal duration, in which acts without religious meaning have their setting. Between these two kinds of time there is, of course, solution of continuity; but by means of rites religious man can pass without danger from ordinary temporal duration to sacred time.

One essential difference between these two qualities of time strikes us immediately: *by its very nature sacred time is reversible* in the sense that, properly speaking, it is *a primordial mythical time made present*. Every religious festival, any liturgical time, represents the reactualization of a sacred event that took place in a mythical past, "in the beginning." Religious participation in a festival implies emerging from ordinary temporal duration and reintegration of the mythical time reactualized by the festival itself. Hence sacred time is indefinitely recoverable, indefinitely repeatable. From one point of view it could be said that it does not "pass," that it does not constitute an irreversible duration. It is an ontological, Parmenidean time; it always remains equal to itself, it neither changes nor is exhausted. With each periodical festival, the participants find the same sacred time—the same that had been manifested in the festival of the previous year or in the festival of a century earlier; it is the time that was created and sanctified by the gods at the period of their *gesta*, of which the festival is precisely a reactualization. In other words the participants in the festival meet in it *the first appearance of sacred time*, as it appeared *ab origine, in illo tempore*. For the sacred time in which the festival runs its course did not exist before the divine *gesta* that the festival commemorates. By creating the various realities that today constitute the world, the gods *also founded sacred time*, for the time contemporary with a creation was necessarily sanctified by the presence and activity of the gods.

Hence religious man lives in two kinds of time, of which the more important, sacred time, appears under the paradoxical aspect of a circular time, reversible and recoverable, a sort of eternal mythical present that is periodically reintegrated by means of rites. This attitude in regard to time suffices to distinguish religious from nonreligious man; the former refuses to live solely in what, in modern terms, is called the historical present; he attempts to regain a sacred time that, from one point of view, can be homologized to eternity.

What time is for the nonreligious man of modern societies would be more difficult to put into a few words. We do not intend to discuss the modern philosophies of time nor the concepts that modern science uses in its own investigations. Our aim is to compare not systems or philosophies but existential attitudes and behaviors. Now, what it is possible to observe in respect to a non-religious man is that he too experiences a certain discontinuity and heterogeneity of time. For him too there is the comparatively monotonous time of his work, and the time of celebrations and spectacles—in short, "festal time." He too lives in varying temporal rhythms and is aware of times of different intensities; when he is listening to the kind of music that he likes or, being in love, waits for or meets his sweetheart, he obviously experiences a different temporal rhythm from that which he experiences when he is working or bored.

But, in comparison with religious man, there is an essential difference. The latter experiences intervals of time that are "sacred," that have no part in the temporal duration that precedes and follows them, that have a wholly different structure and origin, for they are of a primordial time, sanctified by the gods and capable of being made present by the festival. This transhuman quality of liturgical time is inaccessible to a nonreligious man. This is as much as to say that, for him, time can present neither break nor mystery; for him, time constitutes man's deepest existential dimension; it is linked to his own life, hence it has a beginning and an end, which is death, the annihilation of his life. However many the temporal rhythms that he experiences, however great their differences in intensity, nonreligious man knows that they always represent a human experience, in which there is no room for any divine presence.

For religious man, on the contrary, profane temporal duration can be periodically arrested; for certain rituals have the power to interrupt it by periods of a sacred time that is nonhistorical (in the sense that it does not belong to the historical present). Just as a church constitutes a break in plane in the profane space of a modern city, the service celebrated inside it marks a break in profane temporal duration. It is no longer today's historical time that is present—the time that is experienced, for example, in the adjacent streets—but the time in which the historical existence of Jesus Christ occurred, the time sanctified by his preaching, by his passion, death, and resurrection. But we must add that this example does not reveal all the difference between sacred and profane time; Christianity radically changed the experience and the concept of liturgical time, and this is due to the fact that Christianity affirms the historicity of the person of Christ. The Christian liturgy unfolds in *a historical time sanctified by the incarnation of the Son of God*. The sacred time periodically reactualized in pre-Christian religions (especially in the archaic religions) is a *mythical time*, that is, a primordial time, not to be found in the historical past, an *original time*, in the sense that it came into existence all at once, that it was not preceded by another time, because no time could exist *before the appearance of the reality narrated in the myth*.

It is this archaic conception of mythical time that is of chief concern to us. We shall later see how it differs from the conceptions held by Judaism and Christianity.

TEMPLUM-TEMPUS

We shall begin our investigation by presenting certain facts that have the advantage of immediately revealing religious man's behavior in respect to time. First of all, an observation that is not without importance: in a number of North American Indian languages the term world (= Cosmos) is also used in the sense of year. The Yokuts say "the world has passed," meaning "a year has gone by." For the Yuki, the year is expressed by the words for earth or world. Like the Yokuts, they say "the world has passed" when a year has passed. This vocabulary reveals the intimate religious connection between the world and cosmic time. The cosmos is conceived as a living unity that is born, develops, and dies on the last day of the year, to be reborn on New Year's Day. We shall see that this *rebirth* is a *birth*, that the cosmos is reborn each year because, at every New Year, time begins *ab initio*.

The intimate connection between the cosmos and time is religious in nature: the cosmos is homologizable to cosmic time (= the Year) because they are both sacred realities, divine creations. Among some North American peoples this cosmic-temporal connection is revealed even in the structure of sacred buildings. Since the temple represents the image of the world, it can also comprise a temporal symbolism. We find this, for example, among the Algonquins and the Sioux. As we saw, their sacred lodge represents the universe; but at the same time it symbolizes the year. For the year is conceived as a journey through the four cardinal directions, signified by the four doors and four windows of the lodge. The Dakotas say: "The Year is a circle around the world"—that is, around their sacred lodge, which is an *imago mundi*.[1]

A still clearer example is found in India. We saw that the erection of an altar is equivalent to a repetition of the cosmogony. The texts add that "the fire altar is the year" and explain its temporal system as follows: the 360 bricks of the enclosure correspond to the 360 nights of the year, and the 360 *yajusmati* bricks to the 360 days (*Shatapatha Brāhmana*, X, 5, 4, 10; etc.). This is as much as to say that, with the building of each fire altar, not only is the world remade but the year is built too; in other words, *time is regenerated by being created anew*. But then, too, the year is assimilated to Prajāpati, the cosmic god; consequently, with each new altar Prajāpati is reanimated—that is, the sanctity of the world is strengthened. It is not a matter of profane time, of mere temporal duration, but of the sanctification of cosmic time. What is sought by the erection of the fire altar is to sanctify the world, hence to place it in a sacred time.

We find a similar temporal symbolism as part of the

[1] Werner Müller, *Die blaue Hütte*, Wiesbaden, 1954, p. 133.

cosmological symbolism of the Temple at Jerusalem. According to Flavius Josephus (*Ant. Jud.*, III, 7, 7), the twelve loaves of bread on the table signified the twelve months of the year and the candelabrum with seventy branches represented the decans (the zodiacal division of the seven planets into tens). The Temple was an *imago mundi*; being at the Center of the World, at Jerusalem, it sanctified not only the entire cosmos but also cosmic life—that is, time.

Hermann Usener has the distinction of having been the first to explain the etymological kinship between *templum* and *tempus* by interpreting the two terms through the concept of "intersection," (*Schneidung, Kreuzung*).[2] Later studies have refined the discovery: "*templum* designates the spatial, *tempus* the temporal aspect of the motion of the horizon in space and time."[3]

The underlying meaning of all these facts seems to be the following: for religious man of the archaic cultures, *the world is renewed annually*; in other words, *with each new year it recovers* its original sanctity, the sanctity that it possessed when it came from the Creator's hands. This symbolism is clearly indicated in the architectonic structure of sanctuaries. Since the temple is at once the holy place par excellence and the image of the world, it sanctifies the entire cosmos and also sanctifies cosmic life. This cosmic life was imagined in the form of a

[2] H. Usener, *Götternamen*, 2nd. ed., Bonn, 1920, pp. 191 ff.

[3] Werner Müller, *Kreis und Kreuz*, Berlin, 1938, p. 39; cf. also pp. 33 ff.

circular course; it was identified with the year. The year was a closed circle; it had a beginning and an end, but it also had the peculiarity that it could be reborn in the form of a *new* year. With each New Year, a time that was "new," "pure," "holy"—because not yet worn —came into existence.

But time was reborn, began again, because with each New Year the world was created anew. In the preceding chapter we noted the considerable importance of the cosmogonic myth as paradigmatic model for every kind of creation and construction. We will now add that the cosmogony equally implies the creation of time. Nor is this all. For just as the cosmogony is the archetype of all creation, cosmic time, which the cosmogony brings forth, is the paradigmatic model for all other times— that is, for the times specifically belonging to the various categories of existing things. To explain this further: for religious man of the archaic cultures, every creation, every existence begins in time; *before a thing exists, its particular time could not exist.* Before the cosmos came into existence, there was no cosmic time. Before a particular vegetable species was created, the time that now causes it to grow, bear fruit, and die did not exist. It is for this reason that every creation is imagined as having taken place *at the beginning of time, in principio.* Time gushes forth with the first appearance of a new category of existents. This is why myth plays such an important role; as we shall show later, the way in which a reality came into existence is revealed by its myth.

ANNUAL REPETITION OF THE CREATION

It is the cosmogonic myth that tells how the cosmos came into existence. At Babylon during the course of the *akītu* ceremony, which was performed during the last days of the year that was ending and the first days of the New Year, the *Poem of Creation*, the *Enuma elish*, was solemnly recited. This ritual recitation reactualized the combat between Marduk and the marine monster Tiamat, a combat that took place *ab origine* and put an end to chaos by the final victroy of the god. Marduk created the cosmos from Tiamat's dismembered body and created man from the blood of the demon Kingu, Tiamat's chief ally. That this commemoration of the Creation was in fact a *reactualization* of the cosmogonic act is shown both by the rituals and in the formulas recited during the ceremony.

The combat between Tiamat and Marduk, that is, was mimed by a battle between two groups of actors, a ceremonial that we find again among the Hittites (again in the frame of the dramatic scenario of the New Year), among the Egyptians, and at Ras Shamra. The battle between two groups of actors *repeated the passage from chaos to cosmos*, actualized the cosmogony. The mythical event became *present* once again. "May he continue to conquer Tiamat and shorten his days!" the priest cried. The combat, the victory, and the Creation took place *at that instant, hic et nunc.*

Since the New Year is a reactualization of the cosmogony, it implies *starting time over again at its begin-ning*, that is, restoration of the primordial time, the "pure" time, that existed at the moment of Creation. This is why the New Year is the occasion for "purifica-tions," for the expulsion of sins, of demons, or merely of a scapegoat. For it is not a matter merely of a certain temporal interval coming to its end and the beginning of another (as a modern man, for example, thinks); it is also a matter of abolishing the past year and past time. Indeed, this is the meaning of ritual purifications; there is more than a mere "purification"; the sins and faults of the individual and of the community as a whole are annulled, *consumed as by fire.*

The Nawrōz—the Persian New Year—commemorates the day that witnessed the creation of the world and man. It was on the day of Nawrōz that the "renewal of the Creation" was accomplished, as the Arabic historian al-Bīrūnī expressed it. The king proclaimed: "Here is a new day of a new month of a new year; what time has worn must be renewed." Time had worn the human being, society, the cosmos—and this destructive time was profane time, duration strictly speaking; it had to be abolished in order to reintegrate the mythical moment in which the world had come into existence, bathed in a "pure," "strong," and sacred time. The abolition of pro-fane past time was accomplished by rituals that signified a sort of "end of the world." The extinction of fires, the return of the souls of the dead, social confusion of the type exemplified by the Saturnalia, erotic license, orgies, and so on, symbolized the retrogression of the cosmos into chaos. On the last day of the year the universe was dissolved in the primordial waters. The marine monster Tiamat—symbol of darkness, of the formless, the non-manifested—revived and once again threatened. The world that had existed for a whole year *really* disappeared. Since Tiamat was again present, the cosmos was annulled; and Marduk was obliged to create it once again, after having once again conquered Tiamat.[4]

The meaning of this periodical retrogression of the world into a chaotic modality was this: all the "sins" of the year, everything that time had soiled and worn, was annihilated in the physical sense of the word. By symbolically participating in the annihilation and re-creation of the world, man too was created anew; he was reborn, for he began a new life. With each New Year, man felt freer and purer, for he was delivered from the burden of his sins and failings. He had reintegrated the fabulous time of Creation, hence a sacred and strong time—sacred because transfigured by the presence of the gods, strong because it was the time that belonged, and belonged only, to the most gigantic creation ever accomplished, that of the universe. Symbolically, man became contemporary with the cosmogony, he was present at the creation of the world. In the ancient Near East,

4 For New Year rituals, cf. *Myth*, pp. 55 ff.

he even participated actively in its creation (cf. the two opposed groups, representing the god and the marine monster).

It is easy to understand why the memory of that marvelous time haunted religious man, why he periodically sought to return to it. *In illo tempore* the gods had displayed their greatest powers. *The cosmogony is the supreme divine manifestation,* the paradigmatic act of strength, superabundance, and creativity. Religious man thirsts for the real. By every means at his disposal, he seeks to reside at the very source of primordial reality, when the world was *in statu nascendi.*

REGENERATION THROUGH RETURN TO THE TIME OF ORIGINS

All this would warrant detailed study, but for the moment only two features will occupy our attention: (1) through annual repetition of the cosmogony, time was regenerated, that is, it began again as sacred time, for it coincided with the *illud tempus* in which the world had first come into existence; (2) by participating ritually in the end of the world and in its re-creation, any man became contemporary with the *illud tempus*; hence he was born anew, he began life over again with his reserve of vital forces *intact,* as it was at the moment of his birth.

These facts are important; they reveal the secret of

religious man's attitude and behavior in respect to time. Since the sacred and strong time is the *time of origins*, the stupendous instant in which a reality was created, was for the first time fully manifested, man will seek periodically to return to that original time. This ritual reactualizing of the *illud tempus* in which the first epiphany of a reality occurred is the basis for all sacred calendars; the festival is not merely the commemoration of a mythical (and hence religious) event; it *reactualizes* the event.

The paramount *time of origins* is the time of the cosmogony, the instant that saw the appearance of the most immense of realities, the world. This, as we saw in the preceding chapter, is the reason the cosmogony serves as the paradigmatic model for every creation, for every kind of doing. It is for this same reason that *cosmogonic time* serves as the model for all *sacred times*; for if sacred time is that in which the gods manifested themselves and created, obviously the most complete divine manifestation and the most gigantic creation is the creation of the world.

Consequently, religious man reactualizes the cosmogony not only each time he creates something (his "own world"—the inhabited territory—or a city, a house, etc.), but also when he wants to ensure a fortunate reign for a new sovereign, or to save threatened crops, or in the case of a war, a sea voyage, and so on. But, above all, the ritual recitation of the cosmogonic myth plays an important role in healing, when what is sought is the *regeneration* of the human being. In Fiji, the ceremony for installing a new ruler is called creation of the world, and the same ceremony is repeated to save threatened crops. But it is perhaps Polynesia that exhibits the widest application of the cosmogonic myth. The words that Io spoke *in illo tempore* to create the world have become ritual formulas. Men repeat them on many occasions— to fecundate a sterile womb, to heal (mental as well as physical ailments), to prepare for war, but also on the occasion of a death or to stimulate poetic inspiration.[5]

Thus the cosmogonic myth serves the Polynesians as the archetypal model for all creations, on whatever plane —biological, psychological, spiritual. But since ritual recitation of the cosmogonic myth implies reactualization of that primordial event, it follows that he for whom it is recited is magically projected *in illo tempore*, into the "beginning of the World"; he becomes contemporary with the cosmogony. What is involved is, in short, a return to the original time, the therapeutic purpose of which is to begin life once again, a symbolic rebirth. The conception underlying these curative rituals seems to be the following: life cannot be repaired, it can only be recreated through symbolic repetition of the cosmogony, for, as we have said, the cosmogony is the paradigmatic model for all creation.

[5] Cf. the bibliographical reference in *Myth*, pp. 82 ff. and in *Patterns*, p. 410.

The regenerative function of the return to the time of origins becomes still more clear if we make a detailed examination of an archaic therapy, such, for example, as that of the Na-khi, a Tibeto-Burmese people living in Southwest China (Yün-nan Province). The therapeutic ritual proper consists in the solemn recitation of the myth of the creation of the world, followed by myths of the origin of maladies from the wrath of the snakes and the appearance of the first Shaman-Healer who brought humanity the necessary medicines. Almost all the rituals invoke the mythical *beginning*, the mythical *illud tempus*, when the world was not yet made: "In the beginning, at the time when the heavens, sun, moon, stars, planets and the land had not yet appeared, when nothing had yet come forth," etc. Then comes the cosmogony and the appearance of the snakes: "At the time when heaven came forth, the sun, moon, stars and planets, and the earth was spread out; when the mountains, valleys, trees and rocks came forth . . . at that time there came forth the Nāgas and dragons," etc. The birth of the First Healer and the appearance of medicines is then narrated. After this it is said: "Unless its origin is related one should not speak about it."[6]

The important fact to be noted in connection with these magical healing chants is that *the myth of the origin of the medicines employed* is always incorporated into the

[6] J. F. Rock, *The Na-khi Nāga Cult and Related Ceremonies*, Rome, 1952, Vol. II, pp. 279 ff.

cosmogonic myth. It is well known that in all primitive and traditional therapies a remedy becomes efficacious only if its origin is ritually rehearsed in the sick person's presence. A large number of Near Eastern and European incantations contain the history of the sickness or of the demon who has provoked it, at the same time that they evoke the mythical moment in which a divinity or a saint succeeded in conquering the malady. But we consider it certain that the origin myth was copied after the cosmogonic myth, for the latter is the paradigmatic model for all origins. This, moreover, is why, in therapeutic incantations, the origin myth is often preceded by the cosmogonic myth and even incorporated into it. An Assyrian incantation against toothache rehearses that "after Anu made the heavens, the heavens made the earth, the earth made the rivers, the rivers made the canals, the canals made the pools, the pools made the worm." And the worm goes "weeping" to Shamash and Ea and asks them what will be given it to eat, to destroy. The gods offer it fruits, but the worm asks them for human teeth. "Since thou hast spoken thus, O Worm, may Ea break thee with his powerful hand!"[7] Here are presented: (1) the creation of the world; (2) the birth of the worm and of the sickness; (3) the primordial and paradigmatic gesture of healing (Ea's destruction of the worm). The

---

[7] Campbell Thompson, *Assyrian Medical Texts*, London, 1932, p. 59. Cf. also Eliade, "Kosmogonische Mythen und magische Heilungen," *Paideuma*, 1956, pp. 194-204.

therapeutic efficacy of the incantation lies in the fact that, ritually uttered, it reactualizes the mythical time of origins, both the origin of the world and the origin of toothaches and their treatment.

FESTIVAL TIME
AND THE STRUCTURE OF FESTIVALS

The *time of origin* of a reality—that is, the time inaugurated by the first appearance of the reality—has a paradigmatic value and function; that is why man seeks to reactualize it periodically by means of appropriate rituals. But the "first manifestation" of a reality is equivalent to its *creation* by divine or semidivine beings; hence, recovering this *time of origin* implies ritual repetition of the gods' creative act. The periodic reactualization of the creative acts performed by the divine beings *in illo tempore* constitutes the sacred calendar, the series of festivals. A festival always takes place in the original time. It is precisely the reintegration of this original and sacred time that differentiates man's behavior *during* the festival from his behavior *before* or *after* it. For in many cases the same acts are performed during the festival as during nonfestival periods. But religious man believes that he then lives in *another* time, that he has succeeded in returning to the mythical *illud tempus*.

During their annual totemic ceremony, the *Intichiuma,*

the Australian Arunta repeat the journey taken by the particular clan's divine Ancestor in the mythical time (*alcheringa*, literally, the dream time). They stop at all the countless places at which the Ancestor stopped and repeat the same acts and gestures that he performed *in illo tempore*. During the entire ceremony they fast, carry no weapons, and avoid all contact with their women and with members of other clans. They are completely immersed in the dream time.[8]

The festivals annually celebrated in a Polynesian island, Tikopia, reproduce the "works of the Gods"—that is, the acts by which in the mythical time the gods fashioned the world as it is today.[9] The festival time in which the Tikopia live during the ceremonies is characterized by certain prohibitions (*tabus*): noise, games, dancing cease. The passage from profane to sacred time is indicated by ritually cutting a piece of wood in two. The numerous ceremonies that make up the periodical festivals—and which, once again, are only the reiteration of the paradigmatic acts of the gods—*seem* not to be different from normal activities; they comprise ritual repairing of boats, rites relative to the cultivation of food plants (yam, taro, etc.), repairing of sanctuaries. But in reality all these ceremonial activities differ from similar labors performed at ordinary times by the fact

[8] F. J. Gillen, *The Native Tribes of Central Australia*, 2nd ed., London, 1938, pp. 170 ff.

[9] Cf. Raymond Firth, *The Work of the Gods in Tikopia*, I, London, 1940.

that they are performed on *only a few objects* (which in some sort constitute the archetypes of their respective classes) and also because the ceremonies take place in an atmosphere saturated with the sacred. The natives, that is, are conscious that they are reproducing, to the smallest detail, the paradigmatic acts of the gods as they were performed *in illo tempore.*

This is as much as to say that religious man periodically becomes the contemporary of the gods in the measure in which he reactualizes the primordial time in which the divine works were accomplished. On the level of primitive civilizations, whatever man does has a transhuman model; hence, even outside of the festival time, his acts and gestures imitate the paradigmatic models established by the gods and the mythical ancestors. But this imitation is likely to become less and less accurate. The model is likely to be distorted or even forgotten. It is the periodical reactualizations of the divine acts—in short, the religious festivals—that restore human knowledge of the sacrality of the models. The ritual repairing of ships and the ritual cultivation of the yam no longer resemble the similar operations performed outside of the sacred periods. For one thing, they are more precise, closer to the divine models; for another, they are *ritual* —that is, their intent is religious. A boat is repaired ceremonially not because it is in need of repair but because, *in illo tempore,* the gods showed men how to repair boats. It is a case not of an empirical operation but of a religious act, an *imitatio dei*. The object repaired is no longer one of the many objects that constitute the class "boats" but a mythical archetype—*the very boat that the gods manipulated in illo tempore*. Hence the time in which the ritual repairing of boats is performed coheres with primordial time; it is the same time in which the gods labored.

Obviously, not all varieties of periodical festivals can be reduced to the type just examined. But it is not with the morphology of the festival that we are concerned; it is with the structure of the sacred time actualized in festivals. It can be said of sacred time that it is always the same, that it is "a succession of eternities" (Hubert and Mauss). For, however complex a religious festival may be, it always involves a sacred event that took place *ab origine* and that is ritually made present. The participants in the festival become contemporaries of the mythical event. In other words, they emerge from their historical time—that is, from the time constituted by the sum total of profane personal and intrapersonal events —and recover primordial time, which is always the same, which belongs to eternity. Religious man periodically finds his way into mythical and sacred time, re-enters the *time of origin*, the time that "floweth not" because it does not participate in profane temporal duration, because it is composed of an *eternal present*, which is indefinitely recoverable.

Religious man feels the need to plunge periodically

into this sacred and indestructible time. For him it is sacred time that makes possible the other time, ordinary time, the profane duration in which every human life takes its course. It is the *eternal present* of the mythical event that makes possible the profane duration of historical events. To give only one example: it is the divine hierogamy, which took place *in illo tempore*, that made human sexual union possible. The union between the god and goddess occurs in an atemporal instant, in an eternal present; sexual unions between human beings—when they are not ritual unions—take place in duration, in profane time. Sacred, mythical time also originates and supports existential, historical time, for it is the latter's paradigmatic model. In short, it is by virtue of the divine or semidivine beings that everything has come into existence. The origin of realities and of life itself is religious. The yam can be cultivated and eaten in the ordinary way because it is periodically cultivated and eaten *ritually*. And these rituals can be performed because the gods revealed them *in illo tempore*, by creating man and the yam and by showing men how to cultivate and eat that particular food plant.

In the festival the sacred dimension of life is recovered, the participants experience the sanctity of human existence as a divine creation. At all other times there is always the danger of forgetting what is fundamental—that existence is not given by what modern men call Nature but is a creation of *Others*, the gods or semidivine beings. But in festivals the participants recover the sacred dimension of existence, by learning again how the gods or the mythical ancestors created man and taught him the various kinds of social behavior and of practical work.

From one point of view this periodical emergence from historical time—and especially the consequences that it has for the total existence of religious man—may appear to be a refusal of history, hence a refusal of creative freedom. After all, what is involved is an eternal return *in illo tempore*, to a past that is mythical, completely unhistorical. It could be concluded that this eternal repetition of the paradigmatic acts and gestures revealed by the gods *ab origine* is opposed to any human progress and paralyzes any creative spontaneity. Certainly, the conclusion is justifiable in part. But only in part. For religious man, even the most primitive, does not refuse progress in principle; he accepts it but at the same time bestows on it a divine origin and dimension. Everything that from the modern point of view seems to us to have signified progress (of whatever kind— whether social, cultural, technical, etc.) in comparison with a previous situation, all this the various primitive societies have accepted in the course of their long history as a series of new divine revelations. But for the moment we shall leave this aspect of the problem aside. What is of primary importance to us is to understand the religious meaning of this repetition of divine acts and gestures. Now, it seems obvious that, if religious man feels the need of indefinitely reproducing the same paradigmatic acts and gestures, *this is because he desires and attempts to live close to his gods.*

PERIODICALLY BECOMING CONTEMPORARY WITH THE GODS

In the preceding chapter, when we studied the cosmological symbolism of cities, temples, and houses, we showed that it is bound up with the idea of a Center of the World. The religious symbolism implicit in the symbolism of the center appears to be this: man desires to have his abode in a space opening upward, that is, communicating with the divine world. To live near to a Center of the World is, in short, equivalent to living as close as possible to the gods.

We find the same desire for a close approach to the gods if we analyze the meaning of religious festivals. To reintegrate the sacred time of origin is equivalent to becoming contemporary with the gods, hence to living in their presence—even if their presence is mysterious in the sense that it is not always visible. The intention that can be read in the experience of sacred space and sacred time reveals a desire to reintegrate a primordial situation—that in which the gods and the mythical ancestors were *present*, that is, were engaged in creating the world, or in organizing it, or in revealing the foundations of civilization to man. This primordial situation is not historical, it is not calculable chronologically; what is involved is a mythical anteriority, the time of origin, what took place "in the beginning," *in principio.*

Now, what took place "in the beginning" was this: the divine or semidivine beings were active on earth. Hence the nostalgia for origins is equivalent to a *religious* nostalgia. Man desires to recover the active presence of the gods; he also desires to live in the world as it came from the Creator's hands, fresh, pure, and strong. It is the nostalgia for the *perfection of beginnings* that chiefly explains the periodical return *in illo tempore.* In Christian terms, it could be called a nostalgia for paradise, although on the level of primitive cultures the religious and ideological context is entirely different from that of Judaeo-Christianity. But the mythical time whose reactualization is periodically attempted is a time sanctified by the divine presence, and we may say that the desire to live in *the divine presence* and in *a perfect world* (perfect because newly born) corresponds to the nostalgia for a paradisal situation.

As we noted above, this desire on the part of religious man to travel *back* periodically, his effort to reintegrate a mythological situation (the situation as it was in the *beginning*) may appear intolerable and humiliating to modern eyes. Such a nostalgia inevitably leads to the continual repetition of a limited number of gestures and patterns of behavior. From one point of view it may even be said that religious man—especially the religious man of primitive societies—is above all a man paralyzed by the myth of the eternal return. A modern psychologist would be tempted to interpret such an attitude as anxiety before the danger of the new, refusal to assume responsibility for a genuine historical existence, nostalgia for a situation that is paradisal precisely because it is embryonic, insufficiently detached from nature.

That problem is too complex to be discussed here. In any case, it lies outside the field of our investigation, for, in the last analysis, it implies the problem of the opposition between premodern and modern man. Let us rather say that it would be wrong to believe that the religious man of primitive and archaic societies refuses to assume the responsibility for a genuine existence. On the contrary, as we have seen and shall see again, he courageously assumes immense responsibilities—for example, that of collaborating in the creation of the cosmos, or of creating his own world, or of ensuring the life of plants and animals, and so on. But it is a different kind of responsibility from those that, to us moderns, appear to be the only genuine and valid responsibilities. It is *a responsibility on the cosmic plane*, in contradistinction to the moral, social, or historical responsibilities that are alone regarded as valid in modern civilizations. From the point of view of profane existence, man feels no responsibility except to himself and to society. For him, the universe does not properly constitute a cosmos

—that is, a living and articulated unity; it is simply the sum of the material reserves and physical energies of the planet, and the great concern of modern man is to avoid stupidly exhausting the economic resources of the globe. But, existentially, the primitive always puts himself in a cosmic context. His personal experience lacks neither genuineness nor depth; but the fact that it is expressed in a language unfamiliar to us makes it appear spurious or infantile to modern eyes.

To revert to our immediate subject: we have no warrant for interpreting periodic return to the sacred time of origin as a rejection of the real world and an escape into dream and imagination. On the contrary, it seems to us that, here again, we can discern the *ontological obsession* to which we have referred and which, moreover, can be considered an essential characteristic of the man of the primitive and archaic societies. For to wish to reintegrate the *time of origin* is also to wish to return to the *presence of the gods,* to recover the *strong, fresh, pure world* that existed *in illo tempore.* It is at once thirst for the *sacred* and nostalgia for *being.* On the existential plane this experience finds expression in the certainty that life can be periodically begun over again with a maximum of good fortune. Indeed, it is not only an optimistic vision of existence, but a total cleaving to being. By all his behavior, religious man proclaims that he believes only in being, and that his participation in being is assured him by the primordial revelation of which he is the guardian. The sum total of primordial revelations is constituted by his myths.

MYTH=PARADIGMATIC MODEL

The myth relates a sacred history, that is, a primordial event that took place at the beginning of time, *ab initio*. But to relate a sacred history is equivalent to revealing a mystery. For the persons of the myth are not human beings; they are gods or culture heroes, and for this reason their *gesta* constitute mysteries; man could not know their acts if they were not revealed to him. The myth, then, is the history of what took place *in illo tempore*, the recital of what the gods or the semidivine beings did at the beginning of time. To tell a myth is to proclaim what happened *ab origine*. Once told, that is, revealed, the myth becomes apodictic truth; it establishes a truth that is absolute. "It is so because it is said that it is so," the Netsilik Eskimos declare to justify the validity of their sacred history and religious traditions. The myth proclaims the appearance of a new cosmic situation or of a primordial event. Hence it is always the recital of a creation; it tells how something was accomplished, began to *be*. It is for this reason that myth is bound up with ontology; it speaks only of *realities*, of what *really* happened, of what was fully manifested.

Obviously these realities are sacred realities, for it is the *sacred* that is pre-eminently the *real*. Whatever belongs to the sphere of the profane does not participate in being, for the profane was not ontologically established by myth, has no perfect model. As we shall soon see, agricultural work is a ritual revealed by the gods or culture heroes. This is why it constitutes an act that is at once *real* and *significant*. Let us think, by comparison, of agricultural work in a desacralized society. Here, it has become a profane act, justified by the economic profit that it brings. The ground is tilled to be exploited; the end pursued is profit and food. Emptied of religious symbolism, agricultural work becomes at once opaque and exhausting; it reveals no meaning, it makes possible no opening toward the universal, toward the world of spirit. No god, no culture hero ever revealed a profane act. Everything that the gods or the ancestors did, hence everything that the myths have to tell about their creative activity, belongs to the sphere of the sacred and therefore participates in *being.* In contrast, what men do on their own initiative, what they do without a mythical model, belongs to the sphere of the profane; hence it is a vain and illusory activity, and, in the last analysis, unreal. The more religious man is, the more paradigmatic models does he possess to guide his attitudes and actions. In other words, the more religious he is, the more does he enter into the *real* and the less is he in danger of becoming lost in actions that, being nonparadigmatic, "subjective," are, finally, aberrant.

This is the aspect of myth that demands particular emphasis here. The myth reveals absolute sacrality, because it relates the creative activity of the gods, unveils the sacredness of their work. In other words, the myth describes the various and sometimes dramatic irruptions of the sacred into the world. This is why, among many primitives, myths cannot be recited without regard for time or place, but only during the seasons that are ritually richest (autumn, winter) or in the course of religious ceremonies—in short, during *a sacred period of time*. It is the irruption of the sacred into the world, an irruption narrated in the myths, that *establishes* the world as a reality. Every myth shows how a reality came into existence, whether it be the total reality, the cosmos, or only a fragment—an island, a species of plant, a human institution. To tell how things came into existence is to explain them and at the same time indirectly to answer another question: *Why* did they come into existence? The why is always implied in the how—for the simple reason that to tell *how* a thing was born is to reveal an irruption of the sacred into the world, and the sacred is the ultimate cause of all real existence.

Moreover, since every creation is a divine work and hence an irruption of the sacred, it at the same time represents an irruption of creative energy into the world. Every creation springs from an abundance. The gods create out of an excess of power, an overflow of energy. Creation is accomplished by a surplus of ontological substance. This is why the myth, which narrates this sacred ontophany, this victorious manifestation of a plenitude of being, becomes the paradigmatic model for all human activities. For it alone reveals the *real,* the superabundant, the effectual. "We must do what the Gods did in the beginning," says an Indian text (*Shatapatha Brāhmana,* VII, 2, 1, 4). "Thus the Gods did; thus men do," the *Taittirīya Brāhmana* adds (I, 5, 9, 4). Hence the supreme function of the myth is to "fix" the paradigmatic models for all rites and all significant human activities—eating, sexuality, work, education, and so on. Acting as a fully responsible human being, man imitates the paradigmatic gestures of the gods, repeats their actions, whether in the case of a simple physiological function such as eating or of a social, economic, cultural, military, or other activity.

In New Guinea a great many myths tell of long sea voyages, thus providing "exemplars for the modern voyagers," as well as for all other activities, "whether of love, or war, or rain-making, or fishing, or whatever else. . . . The narrative gives precedents for the stages of construction, the tabu on sexual intercourse, etc." When a captain goes to sea he personifies the mythical hero Aori. "He wears the costume which Aori is supposed to have worn, with blackened face . . . [and] the same kind of *love* in his hair which Aori plucked from Iviri's head. He dances on the platform and extends his arms like Aori's wings. . . . A man told me that when he went fish shooting (with bow and arrow) he pretended to be Kivavia himself."[10] He did not pray to the mythical

[10] F. E. Williams, cited in Lucien Lévy-Bruhl, *La mythologie primitive,* Paris, 1935, pp. 162, 163-164.

hero for aid and favor; he identified himself with him.

This symbolism of mythical precedents is also found in other primitive cultures. Writing on the Karuk Indians of California, J. P. Harrington says: "Everything that the Karuk did was enacted because the Ikxareyavs were believed to have set the example in story times. The Ikxareyavs were the people who were in America before the Indians came. Modern Karuks, in a quandary now to render the word, volunteer such translations as 'the princes,' 'the chiefs,' 'the angels.' . . . [The Ikxareyavs] remain[ed] with the Karuk only long enough to state and start all customs, telling them in every instance, 'Humans will do the same.' These doings and sayings are still related and quoted in the medicine formulas of the Karuk."[11]

This faithful repetition of divine models has a two-fold result: (1) by imitating the gods, man remains in the sacred, hence in reality; (2) by the continuous reactualization of paradigmatic divine gestures, the world is sanctified. Men's religious behavior contributes to maintaining the sanctity of the world.

REACTUALIZING MYTHS

It is not without interest to note that religious man assumes a humanity that has a transhuman, transcendent model. He does not consider himself to be

[11] J. P. Harrington, cited in *ibid.*, p. 165.

truly man except in so far as he imitates the gods, the culture heroes, or the mythical ancestors. This is as much as to say that religious man wishes to be *other* than he is on the plane of his profane experience. Religious man is not *given;* he *makes* himself, by approaching the divine models. These models, as we said, are preserved in myths, in the history of the divine *gesta.* Hence religious man too regards himself as *made* by history, just as profane man does; but the only history that concerns him is the *sacred history* revealed by the myths—that is, the history of the gods; whereas profane man insists that he is constituted only by human history, hence by the sum of the very acts that, for religious man, are of no importance because they have no divine models. The point to be emphasized is that, from the beginning, religious man sets the model he is to attain on the transhuman plane, the plane revealed by his myths. *One becomes truly a man only by conforming to the teaching of the myths, that is, by imitating the gods.*

We will add that, for the primitives, such an *imitatio dei* sometimes implies a very grave responsibility. We have seen that certain blood sacrifices find their justification in a primordial divine act; *in illo tempore* the god had slain the marine monster and dismembered its body in order to create the cosmos. Man repeats this blood sacrifice—sometimes even with human victims—when he has to build a village, a temple, or simply a house. What the consequences of this *imitatio dei* can be is clearly shown by the mythologies and rituals of numerous primitive peoples. To give only one example: according to the myths of the earliest cultivators, man became what he is today—mortal, sexualized, and condemned to work—in consequence of a primordial murder; *in illo tempore* a divine being, quite often a woman or a maiden, sometimes a child or a man, allowed himself to be immolated in order that tubers or fruit trees should grow from his body. This first murder basically changed the mode of being of human life. The immolation of the divine being inaugurated not only the need to eat but also the doom of death and, in consequence, sexuality, the only way to ensure the continuity of life. The body of the immolated divinity was changed into food; its soul descended under ground, where it established the Land of the Dead. A. E. Jensen, who has devoted an important book to this type of divinities—which he calls *dema* divinities—has conclusively shown that in eating and in dying man participates in the life of the *demas*.[12]

For all these palaeo-agricultural peoples, what is essential is periodically to evoke the primordial event that established the present condition of humanity. Their whole religious life is a commemoration, a remembering. The memory reactualized by the rites (hence by reiterating the primordial murder) plays a decisive role; what happened *in illo tempore* must never be forgotten. The true sin is forgetting. The girl who at

[12] A. E. Jensen, *Das religiöse Weltbild einer frühen Kultur*, Stuttgart, 1948. Jensen borrowed the word *dema* from the Marind-anim of New Guinea.

her first menstruation spends three days in a dark hut without speaking to anyone does so because the murdered maiden, having become the moon, remains three days in darkness; if the menstruating girl breaks the tabu of silence and speaks, she is guilty of forgetting a primordial event. Personal memory is not involved; what matters is to remember the mythical event, the only event worth considering because the only creative event. It falls to the primordial myth to preserve *true history*, the history of the human condition; it is in the myth that the principles and paradigms for all conduct must be sought and recovered.

It is at this stage of culture that we encounter ritual cannibalism. The cannibal's chief concern would seem to be essentially metaphysical; he must not forget what happened *in illo tempore*. Volhardt and Jensen have shown this very clearly; the killing and devouring of sows at festivals, eating the first fruits when tubers are harvested, are *an eating of the divine body, exactly as it is eaten at cannibal feasts*. Sacrifice of sows, head-hunting, cannibalism are symbolically the same as harvesting tubers or coconuts. It is Volhardt's accomplishment to have demonstrated the religious meaning of anthropophagy and at the same time the human responsibility assumed by the cannibal.[13] The food plant is not

[13] E. Volhardt, *Kannibalismus*, Stuttgart, 1939. Cf. Eliade, "Le mythe du bon sauvage ou les prestiges de l'origine," in *id., Mythes, rêves et mystères*, Paris, 1957, pp. 36 ff.

given in nature; it is the product of a slaying, for it was thus that it was created in the dawn of time. Head-hunting, human sacrifices, cannibalism were all accepted by man to ensure the life of plants. Volhardt's insistence on this point is fully justified. The cannibal assumes his responsibility in the world; cannibalism is not a "natural" behavior in primitive man (moreover, it is not found on the oldest levels of culture); it is cultural behavior, based on a religious vision of life. For the vegetable world to continue, man must kill and be killed; in addition, he must assume sexuality to its extreme limit—the orgy. An Abyssinian song declares this: "She who has not yet engendered, let her engender; he who has not yet killed, let him kill!" This is a way of saying that the two sexes are doomed to assume their destiny.

Before passing judgment on cannibalism, we must always remember that it was instituted by divine beings. But they instituted it to give human beings the opportunity to assume a responsibility in the cosmos, to enable them to provide for the continuity of vegetable life. The responsibility, then, is religious in nature. The Uito cannibals affirm it: "Our traditions are always alive among us, even when we are not dancing; but we work only that we may dance." Their dances consist in repeating all the mythical events, hence also the first slaying, followed by anthropophagy.

We have cited this example in order to show that, among primitives as in the palaeo-oriental civilizations, the *imitatio dei* is not conceived idyllically, that, on the contrary, it implies an awesome human responsibility. In judging a "savage" society, we must not lose sight of the fact that even the most barbarous act and the most aberrant behavior have divine, transhuman models. To inquire why and in consequence of what degradations and misunderstandings certain religious activities deteriorate and become aberrant is an entirely different problem, into which we shall not enter here. For our purpose, what demands emphasis is the fact that religious man sought to imitate, and believed that he was imitating, his gods even when he allowed himself to be led into acts that verged on madness, depravity, and crime.

SACRED HISTORY, HISTORY, HISTORICISM

Let us recapitulate:

Religious man experiences two kinds of time—profane and sacred. The one is an evanescent duration, the other a "succession of eternities," periodically recoverable during the festivals that made up the sacred calendar. The liturgical time of the calendar flows in a closed circle; it is the cosmic time of the year, sanctified by the works of the gods. And since the most stupendous divine work was the creation of the world, commemoration of the cosmogony plays an important part in many religions. The New Year coincides with the first day of Creation. The year is the temporal dimension of the cosmos. "The world has passed" expresses that a year has run its course.

At each New Year the cosmogony is reiterated, the world re-created, and to do this is also to create time—that is, to regenerate it by beginning it anew. This is why the cosmogonic myth serves as paradigmatic model for every creation or construction; it is even used as a ritual means of healing. By symbolically becoming contemporary with the Creation, one reintegrates the primordial plenitude. The sick man becomes well because he begins his life again with its sum of energy intact.

The religious festival is the reactualization of a primordial event, of a sacred history in which the actors are the gods or semidivine beings. But sacred history is recounted in the myths. Hence the participants in the festival become contemporaries of the gods and the semidivine beings. They live in the primordial time that is sanctified by the presence and activity of the gods. The sacred calendar periodically regenerates time, because it makes it coincide with the *time of origin*, the strong, pure time. The religious experience of the festival—that is, participation in the sacred—enables man periodically to live in the presence of the gods. This is the reason for the fundamental importance of myths in all pre-Mosaic religions, for the myths narrate the *gesta* of the gods and these *gesta* constitute paradigmatic models for all human activities. In so far as he imitates his gods, religious man lives in the *time of origin*, the time of the myths. In other words, he emerges from profane duration to recover an unmoving time, eternity.

Since, for religious man of the primitive societies, myths constitute his sacred history, he must not forget them; by reactualizing the myths, he approaches his gods and participates in sanctity. But there are also tragic divine histories, and man assumes a great responsibility toward himself and toward nature by periodically reactualizing them. Ritual cannibalism, for example, is the consequence of a tragic religious conception.

In short, through the reactualization of his myths, religious man attempts to approach the gods and to participate in *being;* the imitation of paradigmatic divine models expresses at once his desire for sanctity and his ontological nostalgia.

In the primitive and archaic religions the eternal repetition of the divine exploits is justified as an *imitatio dei.* The sacred calendar annually repeats the same festivals, that is, the commemoration of the same mythical events. Strictly speaking, the sacred calendar proves to be the "eternal return" of a limited number of divine *gesta*—and this is true not only for primitive religions but for all others. The festal calendar everywhere constitutes a periodical return of the same primordial situations and hence a reactualization of the same sacred time. For religious man, reactualization of the same mythical events constitutes his greatest hope; for with each reactualization he again has the opportunity to transfigure his existence, to make it like its divine model. In short, for religious man of the primitive and archaic societies, the eternal repetition of paradigmatic gestures and the eternal recovery of the same mythical time of origin, sanctified by the gods, in no sense implies a pessimistic vision of life. On the contrary, for him it is by virtue of this eternal return to the sources of the sacred and the real that human existence appears to be saved from nothingness and death.

The perspective changes completely when the sense of *the religiousness of the cosmos becomes lost.* This is what occurs when, in certain more highly evolved societies, the intellectual élites progressively detach themselves from the patterns of the traditional religion. The periodical sanctification of cosmic time then proves useless and without meaning. The gods are no longer accessible through the cosmic rhythms. The religious meaning of the repetition of paradigmatic gestures is forgotten. But *repetition emptied of its religious content necessarily leads to a pessimistic vision of existence.* When it is no longer a vehicle for reintegrating a primordial situation, and hence for recovering the mysterious presence of the gods, that is, *when it is desacralized,* cyclic time becomes terrifying; it is seen as a circle forever turning on itself, repeating itself to infinity.

This is what happened in India, where the doctrine of cosmic cycles (*yugas*) was elaborately developed. A

complete cycle, a *mahāyuga,* comprises 12,000 years.
It ends with a dissolution, a *pralaya,* which is repeated
more drastically (*mahāpralaya,* the Great Dissolution)
at the end of the thousandth cycle. For the paradigmatic
schema "creation-destruction-creation-etc." is reproduced *ad infinitum.* The 12,000 years of a *mahāyuga*
were regarded as divine years, each with a duration of
360 years, which gives a total of 4,320,000 years for a
single cosmic cycle. A thousand such *mahāyugas* make
up a *kalpa* (form); 14 *kalpas* make up a *manvantāra*
(so named because each *manvantāra* is supposed to be
ruled by Manu, the mythical Ancestor-King.) A *kalpa* is
equivalent to a day in the life of Brahma; a second
kalpa to a night. One hundred of these "years" of
Brahma, in other words 311,000 milliards of human
years, constitute the life of Brahma. But even this duration of the god's life does not exhaust time, for the gods
are not eternal and the cosmic creations and destructions
succeed one another forever.[14]

This is the true eternal return, the eternal repetition of
the fundamental rhythm of the cosmos—its periodical
destruction and re-creation. In short, *it is the primitive
conception of the Year-Cosmos, but emptied of its religious content.* Obviously, the doctrine of *yugas* was
elaborated by intellectual élites, and if it became a pan-
Indian doctrine, we must not suppose that it revealed its

[14] Cf. Eliade, *Myth,* pp. 113 ff.; see also *id., Images et symboles,* Paris,
1952, pp. 80 ff.

terrifying aspect to all the peoples of India. It was chiefly the religious and philosophical élites who felt despair in the presence of cyclic time repeating itself *ad infinitum*. For to Indian thought, this eternal return implied eternal return to existence by force of *karma*, the law of universal causality. Then, too, time was homologized to the cosmic illusion (*māyā*), and the eternal return to existence signified indefinite prolongation of suffering and slavery. In the view of these religious and philosophical élites, the only hope was nonreturn-to-existence, the abolition of karma; in other words, final deliverance (*moksha*), implying a transcendence of the cosmos.[15]

Greece too knew the myth of the eternal return, and the Greek philosophers of the late period carried the conception of circular time to its furthest limits. To quote the perceptive words of H. C. Puech: "According to the celebrated Platonic definition, time, which is determined and measured by the revolution of the celestial spheres, is the moving image of unmoving eternity, which it imitates by revolving in a circle. Consequently all cosmic becoming, and, in the same manner, the duration of this world of generation and corruption in which we live, will progress in a circle or in accordance with an indefinite succession of cycles in the course of which the same reality is made, unmade, and remade in con-

---

[15] This transcendence is achieved through the "fortunate instant" (*kshana*), which implies a sort of sacred Time that permits emergence from time; see *Images et symboles*, pp. 10 ff.

formity with an immutable law and immutable alterna-
tives. Not only is the same sum of existence preserved in
it, with nothing being lost and nothing created, but in
addition certain thinkers of declining antiquity—Pytha-
goreans, Stoics, Platonists—reached the point of admit-
ting that within each of these cycles of duration, of these
aiones, these *aeva*, the same situations are reproduced
that have already been produced in previous cycles and
will be reproduced in subsequent cycles—*ad infinitum*.
No event is unique, occurs once and for all (for example,
the condemnation and death of Socrates), but it has
occurred, occurs, and will occur, perpetually; the same
individuals have appeared, appear, and will reappear at
every return of the cycle upon itself. Cosmic duration is
repetition and *anakuklosis*, eternal return."[16]

Compared with the archaic and palaeo-oriental religions, as well as with the mythic-philosophical conceptions of the eternal return, as they were elaborated in
India and Greece, Judaism presents an innovation of
the first importance. For Judaism, time has a beginning
and will have an end. The idea of cyclic time is left behind. Yahweh no longer manifests himself in *cosmic
time* (like the gods of other religions) but in a *historical
time*, which is irreversible. Each new manifestation of
Yahweh in history is no longer reducible to an earlier
manifestation. The fall of Jerusalem expresses Yahweh's

[16] Henri Charles Puech, "La gnose et le temps," *Eranos-Jahrbuch*, XX,
1952, pp. 60-61.

wrath against his people, but it is no longer the same wrath that Yahweh expressed by the fall of Samaria. His gestures are *personal* interventions in history and reveal their deep meaning *only for his people,* the people that Yahweh had *chosen.* Hence the historical event acquires a new dimension; it becomes a *theophany.*[17]

Christianity goes even further in valorizing *historical time.* Since God was *incarnated,* that is, since he took on *a historically conditioned human existence,* history acquires the possibility of being sanctified. The *illud tempus* evoked by the Gospels is a clearly defined historical time—the time in which Pontius Pilate was Governor of Judaea—but it was *sanctified by the presence of Christ.* When a Christian of our day participates in liturgical time, he recovers the *illud tempus* in which Christ lived, suffered, and rose again—but it is no longer a mythical time, it is the time when Pontius Pilate governed Judaea. For the Christian, too, the sacred calendar indefinitely rehearses the same events of the existence of Christ—but these events took place in history; they are no longer facts that happened at the *origin of time,* "in the beginning." (But we should add that, for the Christian, time begins anew with the birth of Christ, for the Incarnation establishes a new situation of man in the cosmos). This is as much as to say that history reveals itself to be a new dimension of the presence of God

17 Cf. Eliade, *Myth,* pp. 102 ff., on the valorization of history in Judaism, especially by the prophets.

in the world. History becomes *sacred history* once more
—as it was conceived, but in a mythical perspective, in
primitive and archaic religions.[18]

Christianity arrives, not at a *philosophy* but at a *theology* of history. For God's interventions in history, and
above all his Incarnation in the historical person of
Jesus Christ, have a transhistorical purpose—the *salvation* of man.

Hegel takes over the Judaeo-Christian ideology and
applies it to universal history in its totality: the universal
spirit *continually* manifests itself in historical events and
manifests itself *only* in historical events. Thus *the whole*
of history becomes a theophany; everything that has
happened in history *had to happen as it did,* because the
universal spirit so willed it. The road is thus opened to
the various forms of twentieth-century historicistic philosophies. Here our present investigation ends, for all
these new valorizations of time and history belong to
the history of philosophy. Yet we must add that historicism arises as a decomposition product of Christianity; it
accords decisive importance to the historical event
(which is an idea whose origin is Christian) but to the
historical event as such, that is, by denying it any possibility of revealing a transhistorical, soteriological intent.[19]

As for the conceptions of time on which certain his-

18 Cf. Eliade, *Images et symboles,* pp. 222 ff.
19 On the difficulties of historicism, see *Myth,* pp. 147 ff.

toricistic and existentialist philosophies have insisted, the following observation is not without interest: although no longer conceived as a circle, time in these modern philosophies once again wears the terrifying aspect that it wore in the Indian and Greek philosophies of the eternal return. Definitively descralized, time presents itself as a precarious and evanescent duration, leading irremediably to death.

CHAPTER 3

The Sacredness

of Nature

and Cosmic Religion

For religious man, nature is never only "natural"; it is always fraught with a religious value. This is easy to understand, for the cosmos is a divine creation; coming from the hands of the gods, the world is impregnated with sacredness. It is not simply a sacrality *communicated* by the gods, as is the case, for example, with a place or an object consecrated by the divine presence. The gods did more; *they manifested the different modalities of the sacred in the very structure of the world and of cosmic phenomena.*

The world stands displayed in such a manner that, in contemplating it, religious man discovers the many modalities of the sacred, and hence of being. Above all, the world exists, it is there, and it has a structure; it is not a chaos but a cosmos, hence it presents itself as creation, as work of the gods. This divine work always preserves its quality of transparency, that is, it spontaneously reveals the many aspects of the sacred. The sky directly, "naturally," reveals the infinite distance, the transcendence of the deity. The earth too is transparent; it presents itself as universal mother and nurse. The cosmic rhythms manifest order, harmony, permanence, fecundity. The cosmos as a whole is an organism at once *real*, *living*, and *sacred*; it simultaneously reveals the modalities of being and of sacrality. Ontophany and hierophany meet.

In this chapter we shall try to understand how the world presents itself to the eyes of religious man—or, more precisely, how sacrality is revealed through the very structures of the world. We must not forget that for

117

religious man the supernatural is indissolubly connected with the natural, that nature always expresses something that transcends it. As we said earlier: a sacred stone is venerated because it is *sacred,* not because it is a *stone;* it is the sacrality *manifested through the mode of being of the stone* that reveals its true essence. This is why we cannot speak of naturism or of natural religion in the sense that the nineteenth century gave to those terms; for it is "supernature" that the religious man apprehends through the natural aspects of the world.

THE CELESTIAL SACRED
AND THE URANIAN GODS

Simple contemplation of the celestial vault already provokes a religious experience. The sky shows itself to be infinite, transcendent. It is pre-eminently the "wholly other" than the little represented by man and his environment. Transcendence is revealed by simple awareness of infinite height. "Most high" spontaneously becomes an attribute of divinity. The higher regions inaccessible to man, the sidereal zones, acquire the momentousness of the transcendent, of absolute reality, of eternity. There dwell the gods; there a few privileged mortals make their way by rites of ascent; there, in the conception of certain religions, mount the souls of the dead. The "most high" is a dimension inaccessible to man as man; it belongs to superhuman forces and beings. He who ascends by mounting the steps of a sanctuary or the ritual ladder that leads to the sky ceases to be a man; in one way or another, he shares in the divine condition.

All this is not arrived at by a logical, rational operation. The transcendental category of height, of the superterrestrial, of the infinite, is revealed to the whole man, to his intelligence and his soul. It is a total awareness on man's part; beholding the sky, he simultaneously discovers the divine incommensurability and his own situation in the cosmos. For the sky, *by its own mode of being,* reveals transcendence, force, eternity. It *exists absolutely* because it is *high, infinite, eternal, powerful.*

This is the true significance of the statement made above—that the gods manifested the different modalities of the sacred in the very structure of the world. In other words, the cosmos—paradigmatic work of the gods—is so constructed that a religious sense of the divine transcendence is aroused by the very existence of the sky. And since the sky *exists* absolutely, many of the supreme gods of primitive peoples are called by names designating height, the celestial vault, meteorological phenomena, or simply Owner of the Sky or Sky Dweller.

The supreme divinity of the Maori is named Iho; *iho* means elevated, high up. Uwoluwu, the supreme god of the Akposo Negroes, signifies what is on high, the upper regions. Among the Selk'nam of Tierra del Fuego God is called Dweller in the Sky or He Who is in the Sky.

Puluga, the supreme being of the Andaman Islanders, dwells in the sky; the thunder is his voice, wind his breath, the storm is the sign of his anger, for with his lightning he punishes those who break his command-ments. The Sky God of the Yoruba of the Slave Coast is named Olorun, literally Owner of the Sky. The Samoyed worship Num, a god who dwells in the highest sky and whose name means sky. Among the Koryak, the supreme divinity is called the One on High, the Master of the High, He Who Exists. The Ainu know him as the Divine Chief of the Sky, the Sky God, the Divine Creator of the Worlds, but also as *Kamui,* that is, Sky. The list could easily be extended.[1]

We may add that the same situation is found in the religions of more civilized peoples, that is, of peoples who have played an important role in history. The Mongol name for the supreme God is Tengri, which means sky. The Chinese T'ien means at once the sky and the god of the sky. The Sumerian term for divinity, *dingir,* originally meant a celestial epiphany—clear, brilliant. The Babylonian Anu also expresses the idea of sky. The Indo-European supreme god, Diēus, denotes both the celestial epiphany and the sacred (cf. Sanskrit *div,* to shine, day; *dyaus,* sky, day; Dyaus, Indian god of heaven). Zeus and Jupiter still preserve in their names the memory of the sacredness of the sky. The Celtic Taranis (from *taran,* to thunder), the Baltic Perkūnas

[1] Examples and bibliography in Eliade, *Patterns,* pp. 38-67.

(lightning), and the proto-Slavic Perun (cf. Polish *piorun*, lightning) are especially revealing for the later transformations of sky gods into storm gods.[2]

There is no question of naturism here. The celestial god is not identified with the sky, for he is the same god who, creating the entire cosmos, created the sky too. This is why he is called Creator, All-powerful, Lord, Chief, Father, and the like. The celestial god is a person, not a uranian epiphany. But he lives in the sky and is manifested in meteorological phenomena—thunder, lightning, storm, meteors, and so on. This means that certain privileged structures of the cosmos—the sky, the atmosphere—constitute favorite epiphanies of the supreme being; he reveals his presence by what is specifically and peculiarly his—the majesty (*majestas*) of the celestial immensity, the terror (*tremendum*) of the storm.

THE REMOTE GOD

The history of supreme beings whose structure is celestial is of the utmost importance for an understanding of the religious history of humanity as a whole. We cannot even consider writing that history here, in a few pages.[3] But we must at least refer to a fact that to us seems primary. Celestially structured supreme beings

[2] On this see *ibid.*, pp. 66 ff., 79 ff., etc.

[3] For basic data, cf. Eliade, *Patterns*, pp. 38-123. Cf. especially R. Pettazoni, *Dio*, Rome, 1921; *id.*, *L'onniscienza di Dio*, Turin, 1955; Wilhelm Schmidt, *Ursprung der Gottesidee*, I-XII, Münster, 1926-1955.

tend to disappear from the practice of religion, from cult; they depart from among men, withdraw to the sky, and become remote, inactive gods (*dei otiosi*). In short, it may be said of these gods that, after creating the cosmos, life, and man, they feel a sort of fatigue, as if the immense enterprise of the Creation had exhausted their resources. So they withdraw to the sky, leaving a son or a demiurge on earth to finish or perfect the Creation. Gradually their place is taken by other divine figures— the mythical ancestors, the mother-goddesses, the fecundating gods, and the like. The god of the storm still preserves a celestial structure, but he is no longer a creating supreme being; he is only the fecundator of the earth, sometimes he is only a helper to his companion (*paredros*), the earth-mother. The celestially structured supreme being preserves his preponderant place only among pastoral peoples, and he attains a unique situation in religions that tend to monotheism (Ahura-Mazda) or that are fully monotheistic (Yahweh, Allah).

The phenomenon of the remoteness of the supreme god is already documented on the archaic levels of culture. Among the Australian Kulin, the supreme being Bunjil himself created the universe, animals, trees, and man; but after investing his son with power over the earth and his daughter with power over the sky, Bunjil withdrew from the world. He remains among the clouds, like a lord, holding a huge sword. Puluga, the supreme being of the Andaman Islanders, withdrew after creating the world and the first man. The mystery of his remoteness has its counterpart in an almost complete absence of cult; there is no sacrifice, no appeal, no thank offering. The memory of Puluga survives in only a few religious customs—for example, the sacred silence of hunters returning to their village after a successful hunt.

The Dweller in the Sky or He Who Is in the Sky of the Selk'nam is eternal, omniscient, all-powerful, the creator; but the Creation was finished by the mythical ancestors, who had also been made by the supreme god before he withdrew to a place above the stars. For now this god has isolated himself from men, is indifferent to the affairs of the world. He has neither images nor priests. Prayers are addressed to him only in case of sickness. "Thou who art above, take not my child; he is still too young!"[4] Offerings are rarely made to him except during storms.

It is the same among many African peoples; the great celestial god, the supreme being, all-powerful creator, plays only a minor role in the religious life of most tribes. He is too far away or too good to need an actual cult, and he is invoked only in extreme cases. Thus, for example, Θlorun (Owner of the Sky) of the Yoruba, after beginning the Creation of the world, deputed finishing and ruling it to a lower god, Obatala. For his part,

[4] Martin Gusinde, "Das höchste Wesen bei den Selk'nam auf Feuerland," *Festschrift W. Schmidt,* Vienna, 1928, pp. 269-274.

Olorun withdrew from human and earthly affairs, and the supreme god has neither temples nor statues nor priests. Nevertheless, *he is invoked as a last resource in times of calamity.*

Withdrawn into the sky, Ndyambi, the supreme god of the Herero, has abandoned humanity to lower divinites. "Why should we sacrifice to him?" a member of the tribe explained. "We do not need to fear him, for he does not do us any harm, as do the spirits of our dead."[5] The supreme being of the Tukumba is "too great for the common affairs of men."[6] The case is the same with Njankupon among the Tshi-speaking Negroes of West Africa; he has no cult, and homage is paid to him only under unusual circumstances, in case of famines or epidemics or after a violent storm; men then ask him how they have offended him. Dzingbe (the Universal Father), the supreme being of the Ewe, is invoked only during droughts: "O Sky, to whom we owe thanks, great is the drought; make it rain, so that the earth will be refreshed and the fields flourish!"[7] The remoteness and passivity of the supreme being are admirably expressed in a saying of the Gyriama of East Africa, which also describes their god: "Mulugu (God) is up above, the ghosts are down below!"[8] The Bantu say: "God, after creating man,

[5] Cf. Frazer, *The Worship of Nature*, I, London, 1926, pp. 150 ff.

[6] *Ibid.*, p. 185.

[7] J. Spieth, *Die Religion der Eweer*, Göttingen-Leipzig, 1911, pp. 46 ff.

[8] A. Le Roy, *La religion des primitifs*, 7th ed., Paris, 1925, p. 184.

no longer cares about him." And the Negritos repeat: "God has gone far away from us."[9] The Fang peoples of the grasslands of Equatorial Africa sum up their religious philosophy in a song:

> God (Nzame) is above, man below.
> God is God, man is man.
> Each at home, each in his house.[10]

It is useless to multiply examples. Everywhere in these primitive religions the celestial supreme being appears to have lost *religious currency;* he has no place in the cult, and in the myths he draws farther and farther away from man until he becomes a *deus otiosus.* Yet he is remembered and entreated as the last resort, *when all ways of appealing to other gods and goddesses, the ancestors, and the demons, have failed.* As the Oraons express it: "Now we have tried everything, but we still have you to help us." And they sacrifice a white cock to him, crying, "God, thou art our creator, have mercy on us."[11]

THE RELIGIOUS EXPERIENCE OF LIFE

The divine remoteness actually expresses man's increasing interest in his own religious, cultural, and economic discoveries. Through his concern with hierophanies of life, through discovering the sacral fertility

[9] H. Trilles, *Les Pygmées de la Forêt équatoriale,* Paris, 1932, p. 74.
[10] *Ibid.,* p. 77.
[11] Frazer, *op. cit.,* p. 631.

of the earth, and through finding himself exposed to religious experiences that are more concrete (more carnal, even orgiastic), primitive man draws away from the celestial and transcendent god. The discovery of agriculture basically transforms not only primitive man's economy but also and especially his *economy of the sacred*. Other religious forces come into play—sexuality, fertility, the mythology of woman and of the earth, and so on. Religious experience becomes more concrete, that is, more intimately connected with life. The great mother-goddesses and the strong gods or the spirits of fertility are markedly more dynamic and more accessible to men than was the Creator God.

Yet, as we have just seen, in cases of extreme distress, when everything has been tried in vain, and especially in cases of disaster proceeding from the sky—drought, storm, epidemic—men turn to the supreme being again and entreat him. This attitude does not obtain only among primitives. Each time that the ancient Hebrews experienced a period of peace and prosperity, they abandoned Yahweh for the Baals and Astartes of their neighbors. Only historical catastrophes forced them to turn to Yahweh. "And they cried unto the Lord, and said, We have sinned, because we have forsaken the Lord, and have served Baalim and Ashtaroth: but now deliver us out of the hands of our enemies, and we will serve thee" (I Samuel, 12, 10).

The Hebrews turned to Yahweh after historical catastrophes and under the threat of an annihilation determined by history; the primitives remember their supreme beings in cases of cosmic catastrophe. But the meaning of this return to the celestial god is the same in both cases: in an extremely critical situation, in which the very existence of the community is at stake, the divinities who in normal times ensure and exalt life are abandoned in favor of the supreme god. Seemingly, this is a great paradox: the deities that, among the primitives, took the place of the celestially structured gods were—like the Baals and Astartes among the Hebrews—divinities of fertility, of opulence, of fullness of life; in short, divinities that exalted and amplified life, both cosmic life—vegetation, agriculture, cattle—and human life. These divinities seemed to be strong, *powerful*. Their religious currency was explained precisely by their strength, their unlimited vital reserves, their fertility.

And yet their worshippers—primitives and Hebrews alike—had the feeling that all these great goddesses and all these vegetation gods were unable to *save* them, that is, to ensure them existence in really critical moments. These gods and goddesses could only *reproduce* and *augment* life; and they could perform that function only during normal times; in short, they were divinities who governed the cosmic rhythms admirably, but who proved incapable of *saving* the cosmos or human society in moments of crisis (historical crisis among the Hebrews).

The various divinities who took the place of the supreme beings were the repository of the most *concrete* and striking powers, the powers of life. But by that very fact they had become "specialists" in procreation and lost the subtler, nobler, more spiritual powers of the Creator Gods. In discovering the sacredness of life, man let himself be increasingly carried away by his own discovery; he gave himself up to vital hierophanies and turned from the sacrality that transcended his immediate and daily needs.

PERENNIALITY OF CELESTIAL SYMBOLS

Yet we must note that even when the celestial gods no longer dominate religious life, the sidereal regions, uranian symbolism, myths and rites of ascent, and the like, *retain a preponderant place in the economy of the sacred*. What is "above," the "high," continues to reveal the *transcendent* in every religious complex. Driven from the cult and replaced in mythologies by other themes, in the religious life the sky remains ever present by virtue of its symbolism. And this celestial symbolism in turn infuses and supports a number of rites (of ascent, climbing, initiation, royalty, and so on), of myths (the cosmic tree, the cosmic mountain, the chain of arrows connecting earth with heaven, and so on), of legends (*e.g.*, magical flight). The symbolism of the Center of the World—whose immense dissemination we have seen—likewise illustrates the importance of celestial symbolism; for it is at a center that communication with the sky is effected, and the sky constitutes the paradigmatic image of transcendence.

It could be said that the very structure of the cosmos keeps memory of the celestial supreme being alive. It is as if the gods had created the world in such a way that it could not but reflect their existence; for no world is possible without verticality, and that dimension alone is enough to evoke transcendence.

Driven from religious life in the strict sense, the *celestial sacred* remains active through symbolism. A religious symbol conveys its message even if it is no longer *consciously* understood in every part. For a symbol speaks to the whole human being and not only to the intelligence.

STRUCTURE OF AQUATIC SYMBOLISM

Before treating of the earth, we must present the religious valorizations of the waters.[12] There are two reasons for this: (1) The waters existed before the earth (as in Genesis, 1, 2, "Darkness was upon the face of the deep. And the Spirit of God moved upon the face of the waters"). (2) By analyzing the religious values of the waters we shall better grasp the structure and func-

---

[12] On all the following see Eliade, *Patterns*, pp. 188 ff.; *id., Images et symboles*, pp. 199 ff.

tion of symbols. Now, symbolism plays a decisive part in the religious life of humanity; it is through symbols that the world becomes transparent, is able to show the transcendent.

The waters symbolize the universal sum of virtualities; they are *fons et origo*, "spring and origin," the reservoir of all the possibilities of existence; they precede every form and *support* every creation. One of the paradigmatic images of creation is the island that suddenly manifests itself in the midst of the waves. On the other hand, immersion in water signifies regression to the preformal, reincorporation into the undifferentiated mode of pre-existence. *E*mersion repeats the cosmogonic act of formal manifestation; *im*mersion is equivalent to a dissolution of forms. This is why the symbolism of the waters implies both death and rebirth. Contact with water always brings a regeneration—on the one hand because dissolution is followed by a new birth, on the other because immersion fertilizes and multiplies the potential of life. The aquatic cosmology has its counterpart—on the human level—in the hylogenies, the beliefs according to which mankind was born of the waters. The Flood, or the periodical submersion of the continents (myths of the Atlantis type) have their counterpart, on the human level, in man's "second death" (the "dampness" and the *leimon*—the "humid field"—of the Underworld, and so on) or in initiatory death through baptism. But both on the cosmological and the anthropological planes immersion in the waters is equivalent not to a final extinction but to a temporary reincorporation into the indistinct, followed by a new creation, a new life, or a "new man," according to whether the moment involved is cosmic, biological, or soteriological. From the point of view of structure, the flood is comparable to baptism, and the funeral libation to the lustrations of the newborn or to the spring ritual baths that procure health and fertility.

In whatever religious complex we find them, the waters invariably retain their function; they disintegrate, abolish forms, "wash away sins"; they are at once purifying and regenerating. Their destiny is to precede the Creation and to reabsorb it, since they are incapable of transcending their own mode of being, incapable, that is, of manifesting themselves in *forms*. The waters cannot pass beyond the condition of the virtual, of germs and latencies. Everything that is *form* manifests itself above the waters, by detaching itself from the waters.

One point is essential here: both the sacrality of the waters and the structure of aquatic cosmogonies and apocalypses *can be completely revealed only through aquatic symbolism*, which is the only system capable of integrating all of the particular revelations of innumerable hierophanies.[13] This law, moreover, holds for every symbolism; it is the symbolism *as a whole* that valorizes

[13] On this symbolism, cf. Eliade, *Patterns*, pp. 437 ff., especially pp. 448 ff.

the various significations of hierophanies. The Waters of Death, for example, reveal their deeper meaning only to the extent to which the structure of aquatic symbolism is known.

PARADIGMATIC HISTORY OF BAPTISM

The Fathers of the Church did not fail to exploit certain pre-Christian and universal values of aquatic symbolism, although enriching them with new meanings connected with the historical existence of Christ. For Tertullian water, "before all the furnishing of the world, [was] quiescent with God in a yet unshapen state. . . . Water was the first to produce that which had life, that it might be no wonder in baptism if waters knew how to give life. . . . All waters, therefore, in virtue of the pristine privilege of their origin, do, after invocation of God, attain the sacramental power of sanctification; for the Spirit immediately supervenes from the heavens, and rests over the waters, sanctifying them from Himself; and being thus sanctified, they imbibe at the same time the power of sanctifying. . . . They [that] were wont to remedy bodily defects, now heal the spirit; they [that] used to work temporal salvation, now renew eternal" (*De Baptismo*, III-V; trans. S. Thelwal, in *The Writings of . . . Tertullianus*, Edinburgh, 1869, Vol. I, pp. 233-238.).

The "old man" dies through immersion in water, and

gives birth to a new, regenerated being. This symbolism is admirably expressed by John Chrysostom (*Homil. in Joh.*, XXV, 2) who, writing of the multivalence of baptism, says: "It represents death and burial, life and resurrection. . . . When we plunge our heads into the water as into a sepulcher, the old man is immersed, buried wholly; when we come out of the water, the new man appears at the same time."

As we see, the interpretations reached by Tertullian and John Chrysostom are in perfect accord with the structure of aquatic symbolism. *However, into the Christian valorization of the waters there enter certain new elements connected with a "history," specifically with sacred history.* First of all, there is the valorization of baptism as a descent into the abyss of the waters for a combat with the marine monster. This descent has a model—Christ's descent into the Jordan, which was at the same time a descent into the Waters of Death. As Cyril of Jerusalem writes: "According to Job, the dragon Behemoth was in the Waters and received the Jordan into his jaws. Now, since the heads of the dragon must be broken, Jesus, having gone down into the Waters, bound the Strong One, so that we should have the power to walk on scorpions and snakes."[14]

Next comes the valorization of baptism as repetition of the Flood. According to Justin, Christ, a new Noah,

14 Commentary and text in J. Daniélou, *Bible et liturgie*, Paris, 1951, pp. 58 ff.

emerged victorious from the waters to become the head of another race. The Flood figures both the descent into the watery depths and baptism. "The Flood, then, was an image which baptism comes to fulfill. . . . Just as Noah had confronted the Sea of Death in which sinful humanity had been destroyed, and had emerged from it, so the newly baptized man descends into the baptismal piscina to confront the water Dragon in a supreme combat from which he emerges victorious."[15]

But in further connection with the baptismal rite, Christ is also placed in parallel with Adam. The parallel Adam-Christ already has a considerable place in the theology of Saint Paul. "By baptism," Tertullian affirms, "man recovers the likeness of God" (*De Bapt.*, V). For Cyril, "baptism is not only purification from sins and the grace of adoption, but also antitype of the Passion of Christ." Baptismal nudity too bears a meaning that is at once ritual and metaphysical. It is abandoning "the old garment of corruption and sin, which the baptized person takes off in imitation of Christ, the garment with which Adam was clothed after his sin"[16]; but it is also return to primitive innocence, to Adam's state before the fall. "O admirable!" Cyril writes. "Ye were naked before the eyes of all and felt no shame. Because verily ye bear within you the image of the first Adam, who was naked in Paradise, and felt no shame."[17]

---

[15] J. Daniélou, *Sacramentum futuri*, Paris, 1950, p. 65.
[16] J. Daniélou, *Bible et liturgie*, pp. 61, 55.
[17] See also the texts in *ibid.*, pp. 56 ff.

From these few texts, we realize the direction of the Christian innovations. On the one hand, the Fathers sought for correspondences between the two Testaments; on the other, they showed that Jesus had in truth fulfilled God's promises to the people of Israel. But it is important to note that *these new valorizations of baptismal symbolism are nowhere in contradiction to the universally disseminated aquatic symbolism.* Nothing is missing: Noah and the Flood have their counterpart, in countless traditions, in the cataclysm that put an end to a humanity (society) except for one man who would become the mythical Ancestor of a new humanity. The Waters of Death are a leitmotiv of palaeo-oriental, Asiatic, and Oceanic mythologies. Water is pre-eminently the slayer; it dissolves, abolishes all form. It is just for this reason that it is so rich in germs, so creative. No more is baptismal nudity the exclusive property of the Judaeo-Christian tradition; Paradise implies the absence of garments, that is, the absence of attrition, wear (archetypal image of time). All ritual nudity implies an atemporal model, a paradisal image.

The monsters of the abyss recur in many traditions. Heroes, initiates descend into the depths to confront marine monsters; this is a typical initiatory ordeal. To be sure, variants abound in the history of religions: sometimes dragons mount guard over a treasure, sensory image of the sacred, of absolute reality; the ritual (= initiatory) victory over the guardian monster is equivalent to a conquest of immortality.[18] For the Christian, baptism is a sacrament because it was instituted by Christ. But it none the less repeats the initiatory ritual of the ordeal (= fight with the monster), of symbolic death and resurrection (= birth of the new man). We do not say that Judaism or Christianity borrowed these or similar myths and symbols from the religions of neighboring peoples. They had no need to; Judaism inherited both a religious prehistory and a long religious history, in which all these things already existed. It was not even necessary that Judaism should have preserved one or another myth or symbol "awake," in its integrity. It was enough if a group of images survived, even though only obscurely, from pre-Mosaic times. Such images and symbols were capable of recovering a powerful religious currency at any moment.

UNIVERSALITY OF SYMBOLS

Certain Fathers of the primitive Church had seen the value of the correspondence between the symbols advanced by Christianity and the symbols that are the common property of mankind. Addressing those who denied the resurrection of the dead, Theophilus of Antioch appealed to the signs (*tekmēria*) that God had set before them in the great cosmic rhythms—seasons, days, nights. He wrote: "Is there not a resurrection for seeds

[18] On these mythico-ritual motifs, see Eliade, *Patterns,* pp. 207 ff., 283 ff.

and fruits?" For Clement of Rome, "day and night show us the resurrection; night sets, day rises; day departs, night comes."[19]

For the Christian apologists, symbols were pregnant with messages; they *showed* the sacred through the cosmic rhythms. The revelation brought by the faith did not destroy the pre-Christian meanings of symbols; it simply added a new value to them. True enough, for the believer this new meaning eclipsed all the others; it *alone* valorized the symbol, transfigured it into revelation. It was the resurrection of Christ that counted, not the signs that could be read in cosmic life. Yet it remains true that *the new valorization was in some sort conditioned by the very structure of the symbolism*; it could even be said that the aquatic symbol *awaited* the fulfillment of its deepest meaning through the new values contributed by Christianity.

The Christian faith hangs upon a *historical* revelation; it is the incarnation of God in historical time that, in the Christian view, guarantees the validity of symbols. But the universal aquatic symbolism was neither abolished nor dismembered by the historical (= Judaeo-Christian) interpretations of baptismal symbolism. In other words: History cannot basically modify the structure of an archaic symbolism. History constantly adds new meanings, but they do not destroy the structure of the symbol.

19 Cf. L. Beirnaert, "La dimension mythique dans le sacramentalisme chrétien," *Eranos-Jahrbuch*, XVII, 1950, p. 275.

All this is comprehensible if we bear in mind that, for religious man, the world always presents a supernatural valence, that is, it reveals a modality of the sacred. Every cosmic fragment is transparent; its own mode of existence *shows* a particular structure of being, and hence of the sacred. We should never forget that, for religious man, sacrality is a full manifestation of being. The revelations of cosmic sacrality are in some sort primordial revelations; they take place in the most distant religious past of humanity, and the innovations later introduced by history have not had power to abolish them.

TERRA MATER

An Indian prophet, Smohalla, chief of the Wanapum tribe, refused to till the ground. He held that it was a sin to mutilate and tear up the earth, mother of all. He said: "You ask me to plow the ground! Shall I take a knife and tear my mother's bosom? Then when I die she will not take me to her bosom to rest. You ask me to dig for stone! Shall I dig under her skin for her bones? Then when I die, I cannot enter her body to be born again. You ask me to cut grass and make hay and sell it, and be rich like white men! But how dare I cut off my mother's hair?"[20]

[20] James Mooney, "The Ghost-Dance Religion and the Sioux Outbreak of 1890," *Annual Report of the Bureau of American Ethnology*, XIV, 2, Washington, 1896, pp. 721, 724.

These words were spoken scarcely fifty years ago. But they come to us from very far. The emotion that we feel on hearing them arises primarily from their revealing to us, with incomparable freshness and spontaneity, the primordial image of Mother Earth. The image is found throughout the world in countless forms and variants. It is the *Terra Mater* or *Tellus Mater* so familiar to Mediterranean religions, who gives birth to all beings. "Concerning Earth, the mother of all, shall I sing," we read in the Homeric *Hym to Earth*, "firm earth, eldest of gods, that nourishes all things in the world. . . . Thine it is to give or to take life from mortal men" (1 ff.; trans. A. Lang, *Homeric Hymns*, p. 246). And in the *Choephori* Aeschylus celebrates the earth "who bringeth all things to birth, reareth them, and receiveth again into her womb" (127-128; trans. Verrall, '*Choephori'*, p. 214).

The prophet Smohalla does not tell us in what way men are born of the telluric mother. But North American myths reveal how things happened in the beginning, *in illo tempore*. The first men lived for a certain time in the breast of their mother, that is, in the depths of the earth. There in the telluric abyss they led a half-human life; in some sort they were still imperfectly formed embryos. At least so said the Lenni-Lenape or Delaware Indians, who once inhabited Pennsylvania. According to their myths, although the Creator had already prepared on the surface of the earth all the things that men now enjoy there, he had decided that these first men should remain yet a while hidden in the bosom of the telluric mother, so that they might better develop, might ripen. Other American Indian myths speak of an ancient time when Mother Earth brought forth human beings in the same way that she now produces bushes and reeds.[21]

That human beings are born of the earth is a universally disseminated belief.[22] In a number of languages man is called the earthborn. It is believed that children "come" from the depths of the earth, from caverns, caves, ravines, but also from ponds, springs, rivers. In the form of legends, superstitions, or merely as metaphors, such beliefs still survive in Europe. Every district, and almost every town and village, knows of a brook or a spring that "brings" children; they are the *Kinderbrunnen, Kinderteiche, Bubenquellen,* and so on. Even the European of today still preserves an obscure sense of mystical solidarity with his native soil. It is the religious experience of autochthony; the feeling is that of *belonging to a place,* and it is a cosmically structured feeling that goes far beyond family or ancestral solidarity.

The dying man desires to return to Mother Earth, to

---

[21] Cf. Eliade, "La terre-mère et les hiérogamies cosmiques," *Eranos-Jahrbuch,* XXII, 1954, pp. 59 ff.; also in *id., Mythes, rêves et mystères,* pp. 207-252, especially pp. 208 ff.

[22] A. Dieterich, *Mutter Erde,* 3rd ed., Leipzig-Berlin, 1925; B. Nyberg, *Kind und Erde,* Helsinki, 1931; cf. Eliade, *Patterns,* pp. 239 ff.

be buried in his native soil. "Crawl to the Earth, thy mother," says the *Rig Veda* (X, 18, 10). "Thou who art earth, I put thee in the Earth!" we read in the *Atharva Veda* (XVIII, 4, 48). "Let flesh and bones return again to the Earth!" is solemnly intoned at Chinese funeral ceremonies. And Roman sepulchral inscriptions express fear lest the dead man's ashes be buried far from home and, above all, the joy of reincorporating them into the fatherland: *Hic natus hic situs est* (*C.I.L.*, V, 5595: "Here was he born, here is he laid"); *hic situs est patriae* (VIII, 2885: "Here he is laid in his native land"); *hic quo natus fuerat optans erat illo reverti* (V, 1703: "Here where he was born he desired to return").

HUMI POSITIO:
LAYING THE INFANT ON THE GROUND

This fundamental experience—that the human mother is only the representative of the telluric Great Mother—has given rise to countless customs. We will mention, as an example, giving birth on the ground (*humi positio*), a ritual that is found almost all over the world, from Australia to China, from Africa to South America. Among the Greeks and Romans the custom had disappeared by historical times, but there is no doubt that it existed in a more remote past; certain statues of birth goddesses (Eileithia, Damia, Auxeia) represented them on their knees, exactly in the position of a woman giving birth on the ground. In demotic Egyptian texts the expression "to sit on the ground" meant to give birth, childbirth.[23]

The religious meaning of the custom is easy to see: generation and childbirth are microcosmic versions of a paradigmatic act performed by the earth; every human mother only imitates and repeats this primordial act of the appearance of life in the womb of the earth. Hence every mother must put herself in contact with the Great Genetrix, that she may be guided by her in accomplishing the mystery that is the birth of a life, may receive her beneficent energies and secure her maternal protection.

Still more widely disseminated is the laying of the infant on the ground. In some parts of Europe it is still the custom today to lay the infant on the ground as soon as it has been bathed and swaddled. The father then takes the child up from the ground (*de terra tollere*) to show his gratitude. In ancient China "the dying man, like the newborn infant, is laid on the ground. . . . To be born or to die, to enter the living family or the ancestral family (and to leave the one or the other), there is a common threshold, one's native Earth. . . . When the newborn infant or the dying man is laid on the Earth,

[23] Cf. the references in Eliade, "La terre-mère et les hiérogamies cosmiques," in *Mythes, rêves et mystères,* p. 222, n. 1.

it is for her to say if the birth or the death are valid,
if they are to be taken as accomplished and normal facts.
. . . The rite of laying on the Earth implies a substan-
tial identity between the Race and the Soil. And in fact
this idea finds expression in the feeling of autochthony
that is the strongest feeling among those that we can
detect at the beginnings of Chinese history; the idea of
an intimate connection between a country and its inhabi-
tants is a belief so profound that it has remained at the
heart of religious institutions and civil law."[24]

Just as the infant is placed on the ground immediately
after birth so that its true Mother shall legitimize it and
confer her divine protection on it, so, too, infants, children, and grown men are placed on the ground—or
sometimes buried in it—in case of sickness. Symbolic
burial, partial or complete, has the same magico-religious value as immersion in water, baptism. The sick
person is regenerated; he is born anew. The operation
has the same efficacy in wiping out a sin or in curing a
mental malady (the latter representing the same danger
to the collectivity as does crime or somatic sickness).
The sinner is placed in a cask or in a trench dug in the
ground, and when he emerges he is said to "be born a
second time, from his mother's womb." This explains the
Scandinavian belief that a witch can be saved from eter-

[24] Marcel Granet, "Le dépôt de l'enfant sur le sol," *Revue Archéologique,*
1922=*Études sociologiques sur la Chine,* Paris, 1953, pp. 192 ff., 197 ff.

nal damnation if she is buried alive, seed is sown over her, and the resulting crop harvested.[25]

Initiation includes a ritual death and resurrection. This is why, among numerous primitive peoples, the novice is symbolically "killed," laid in a trench, and covered with leaves. When he rises from the grave he is looked upon as a *new man*, for he has been brought to birth once more, this time *directly by the cosmic Mother*.

WOMAN, EARTH, AND FECUNDITY

Woman, then, is mystically held to be one with the earth, childbearing is seen as a variant, on the human scale, of the telluric fertility. All religious experiences connected with fecundity and birth *have a cosmic structure*. The sacrality of woman depends on the holiness of the earth. Feminine fecundity has a cosmic model—that of Terra Mater, the universal Genetrix.

In some religions Mother Earth is imagined as capable of conceiving alone, without the assistance of a coadjutor. Traces of such archaic ideas are still found in the myths of the parthenogenesis of Mediterranean goddesses. According to Hesiod, Gaia (= Earth) gave birth to Ouranos "a being equal to herself, able to cover her completely" (*Theogony*, 126 f.). Other Greek goddesses

---

[25] A. Dieterich, *Mutter Erde*, pp. 28 ff.; B. Nyberg, *Kind und Erde*, p. 150.

likewise gave birth without the help of gods. This is a mythical expression of the self-sufficiency and fecundity of Mother Earth. Such mythical conceptions have their counterparts in beliefs concerning the spontaneous fecundity of woman and in her occult magico-religious powers, which exert a determining influence on plant life. The social and cultural phenomenon known as matriarchy is connected with the discovery of agriculture by woman. It was woman who first cultivated food plants. Hence it is she who becomes owner of the soil and crops.[26] The magico-religious prestige and consequent social predominance of woman have a cosmic model—the figure of Mother Earth.

In other religions the cosmic creation, or at least its completion, is the result of a hierogamy between the Sky-God and Mother Earth. This cosmogonic myth is quite widely disseminated. It is found especially in Oceania—from Indonesia to Micronesia—but it also occurs in Asia, Africa, and the two Americas.[27] Now, as we have seen, the cosmogonic myth is pre-eminently the paradigmatic myth; it serves as model for human behavior. This is why human marriage is regarded as an imitation of the cosmic hierogamy. "I am Heaven," the

[26] J. J. Bachofen, *Das Mutterrecht*, Basel, 1861, 3rd ed. 1948; Wilhelm Schmidt, *Das Mutterrecht*, Vienna, 1955.

[27] Cf. Eliade, *Patterns*, pp. 240 ff. But it should be noted that, although very widely disseminated, the myth of the cosmic hierogamy is not universal and does not appear in the most archaic cultures (Australians, Fuegians, Arctic peoples, etc.).

husband proclaims in the *Brihadāranyaka Upanishad*
(VI, 4, 20), "thou art Earth!" Even so early as the
Atharva Veda (XIV, 2, 71) groom and bride are assimilated to heaven and earth. Dido celebrates her marriage
to Aeneas in the midst of a violent storm (*Aeneid*, IV,
165 ff); their union coincides with that of the elements;
the Sky embraces his wife, dispensing the fertilizing
rain. In Greece marriage rites imitated the example of
Zeus's secret union with Hera (Pausanias, II, 36, 2).
As we should expect, the divine myth is the paradigmatic
model for the human union. But there is another aspect
which requires emphasis—*the cosmic structure of the
conjugal ritual*, and hence of human sexual behavior.
For nonreligious man of the modern societies, this simultaneously *cosmic* and *sacred* dimension of conjugal
union is difficult to grasp. But as we have had occasion
to say more than once, it must not be forgotten that
religious man of the archaic societies sees the world as
fraught with messages. Sometimes the messages are in
cipher, but the myths are there to help man decipher
them. As we shall see later, the whole of human experience can be homologized to cosmic life, hence can be
sanctified, for the cosmos is the supreme creation of the
gods.

Ritual orgies for the benefit of crops likewise have a
divine model—the hierogamy of the Fecundating God
and Mother Earth.[28] The fertility of the fields is stimu-

[28] Cf. Eliade, *Patterns*, pp. 356 ff.

lated by an unlimited genetic frenzy. From one point of view the orgy corresponds to the pre-Creation state of nondifferentiation. This is why certain New Year ceremonies include orgiastic rites: social confusion, sexual license, and saturnalia symbolize regression to the amorphous condition that preceded the Creation of the World. In the case of a creation on the level of vegetable life, this cosmologico-ritual scenario is repeated, for the new crop is equivalent to a new creation. The idea of *renewal*—which we encountered in New Year rituals whose purpose was at once the renewal of time and the regeneration of the world—recurs in orgiastic argricultural scenarios. Here too the orgy is a return to the cosmic night, the preformal, the waters, in order to ensure complete regeneration of life and hence the fertility of the earth and an abundance of crops.

SYMBOLISM OF THE COSMIC TREE AND OF VEGETATION CULTS

As we have just seen, the myths and rites of the Earth-Mother chiefly express ideas of fecundity and abundance. These are religious ideas, for what the various aspects of universal fertility reveal is, in sum, the mystery of generation, of the creation of life. For religious man, the appearance of life is the central mystery of the world. Life comes from somewhere that is not this world and finally departs from here and goes to the beyond, in some mysterious way continues in an unknown place inaccessible to the majority of mortals. Human life is not felt as a brief appearance in time, between one nothingness and another; it is preceded by a pre-existence and continued in a postexistence. Little is known about these two extraterrestrial stages of human life, yet they are known to *exist*. Hence, for religious man, death does not put a final end to life. Death is but another modality of human existence.

All this, moreover, is ciphered in the cosmic rhythms; man need only decipher what the cosmos says in its many modes of being, and he will understand the mystery of life. But one thing seems clear beyond doubt: that the cosmos is a living organism, which renews itself periodically. The mystery of the inexhaustible appearance of life is bound up with the rhythmical renewal of the cosmos. This is why the cosmos was imagined in the form of a gigantic tree; the mode of being of the cosmos, and first of all its capacity for endless regeneration, are symbolically expressed by the life of the tree.

We should note, however, that all this does not represent a mere transposition of images from the microcosmic to the macrocosmic scale. As a natural object, the tree could not suggest *the whole of cosmic life*; on the level of profane experience its mode of being does not coincide with the mode of being of the cosmos in all its complexity. On the level of profane experience vegetable life displays merely a series of births and deaths.

Only the religious vision of life makes it possible to decipher other meanings in the rhythm of vegetation, first of all the ideas of regeneration, of eternal youth, of health, of immortality. The religious idea of *absolute reality*, which finds symbolic expression in so many other images, is also expressed by the figure of a miraculous fruit conferring immortality, omniscience, and limitless power, a fruit that can change men into gods.

The image of the tree was not chosen only to symbolize the cosmos but also to express life, youth, immortality, wisdom. In addition to cosmic trees like the Yggdrasil of Germanic mythology, the history of religions records trees of life (*e.g.*, in Mesopotamia), of immortality (Asia, Old Testament), of knowledge (Old Testament), of youth (Mesopotamia, India, Iran), and so on.[29] In other words, the tree came to express everything that religious man regards as *pre-eminently real and sacred*, everything that he knows the gods to possess of their own nature and that is only rarely accessible to privileged individuals, the heroes and demigods. This is why myths of the quest for youth or immortality give prominent place to a tree with golden fruit or miraculous leaves, a tree growing "in the distant land" (really in the other world) and guarded by monsters (griffins, dragons, snakes). He who would gather its fruits must confront and slay the guardian monster. This in itself tells us

[29] Cf. *ibid.*, pp. 273 ff.; G. Widengren, *The King and the Tree of Life in Ancient Near Eastern Religion*, Uppsala, 1951.

that we here have *an initiatory ordeal of the heroic type;* it is by violence that the victor obtains the superhuman, almost divine condition of eternal youth, invincibility, and unlimited power.

It is in such symbols of a cosmic tree, or tree of immortality or knowledge, that the religious valences of vegetation are expressed with the greatest force and clarity. In other words, the sacred tree or sacred plants display a structure that is not to be seen in the various concrete vegetable species. As we noted before, it is sacrality that unveils the deepest structures of the world. The cosmos appears as a cipher only in the religious perspective. It is for religious man that the rhythms of vegetation simultaneously reveal the mystery of life and creation and the mystery of renewal, youth, and immortality. It could be said that all trees and plants that are regarded as sacred (*e.g.,* the *ashvatha* tree in India) owe their privileged situation to the fact that they incarnate the archetype, the paradigmatic image of vegetation. On the other hand, what causes a plant to be noticed and cultivated is its religious value. According to some writers, all of the plants that are in cultivation today were originally regarded as sacred plants.[30]

What are called vegetation cults do not depend on a profane, "naturistic" experience, connected, for example, with spring and the reawakening of vegetation. On

[30] A. G. Haudricourt and L. Hédin, *L'homme et les plantes cultivées,* Paris, 1946, p. 90.

the contrary, the religious experience of renewal (= re-beginning, re-creation) of the world precedes and justifies the valorization of spring as the resurrection of nature. It is the mystery of the periodical regeneration of the cosmos that is the basis for the religious significance of spring. Then, too, in vegetation cults the emphasis is not always on the natural phenomenon of spring and the appearance of vegetation but on the prophetic *sign* of the cosmic mystery. Bands of young men pay ceremonial visits to the houses of their village and *show* a green branch, a bunch of flowers, a bird.[31] It is the *sign of the imminent resurrection of vegetable life*, testimony that the mystery has been accomplished, that spring will soon come. The majority of these rituals take place *before* the natural phenomenon of spring.

DESACRALIZATION OF NATURE

As we have said before, for religious man nature is never only natural. Experience of a radically desacralized nature is a recent discovery; moreover, it is an experience accessible only to a minority in modern societies, especially to scientists. For others, nature still exhibits a charm, a mystery, a majesty in which it is possible to decipher traces of ancient religious values. No modern man, however irreligious, is entirely insensible to the charms of nature. We refer not only to the

[31] Cf. Eliade, *Patterns*, pp. 316 ff.

esthetic, recreational, or hygienic values attributed to nature, but also to a confused and almost indefinable feeling, in which, however, it is possible to recognize the memory of a debased religious experience.

A definite example of these changes and deteriorations in the religious values of nature will not be without value. We have taken our example from China, for two reasons. (1) In China, as in the West, the desacralization of nature is the work of a minority, especially of the literati; (2) nevertheless in China and in the entire Far East, the process of desacralization has never been carried to its final extreme. Even for the most sophisticated men of letters, "esthetic contemplation" still retains an aura of religious prestige.

From the seventeenth century, arranging gardens in pottery bowls became the fashion among Chinese scholars.[32] The bowls were filled with water, out of which rose a few stones bearing dwarf trees, flowers, and often miniature models of houses, pagodas, bridges, and human figures; they were called "Miniature Mountains" in Annamese and "Artificial Mountains" in Sino-Annamese. These names themselves suggest a cosmological signification; for, as we have seen, the mountain is a symbol of the universe.

But these miniature gardens, which became objects

[32] On the following, cf. Rolf Stein, "Jardins en miniature d'Extrême Orient," *Bulletin de l'École Française d'Extrême Orient*, 42, 1943, pp. 26 ff. and *passim*.

valued by esthetes, had a long history, or even a pre-history, which reveals a profound religious feeling for the world. Their ancestors were bowls whose perfumed water represented the sea and their cover the mountain. The cosmic structure of these objects is obvious. The mystical element was also present, for the mountain in the midst of the sea symbolized the Isles of the Blessed, a sort of Paradise in which the Taoist Immortals lived. So that we have here *a world apart*, a world in miniature, which the scholar set up in his house in order to partake in its concentrated mystical forces, *in order, through meditation, to re-establish harmony with the world*. The mountain was ornamented with grottoes, and the folklore of caves played an important role in the construction of these miniature gardens. Caves are secret retreats, dwell-ings of the Taoist Immortals and places of initiation. They represent a paradisal world and hence are difficult to enter (symbolism of the "narrow gate," to which we shall return in the next chapter).

But this whole complex—water, trees, mountain, grotto—which had played such a considerable role in Taoism was only the development of a still older reli-gious idea: that of the *perfect place*, combining *com-pleteness* (mountain and water) with *solitude*, and thus *perfect* because at once the world in miniature and Para-dise, source of bliss and place of immortality. But the perfect landscape—mountain and water—was only the immemorial sacred place where, in China, at every returning spring, youths and girls met to intone alternating ritual chants and for amorous encounters. It is possible to divine the successive valorizations of the primordial sacred place. In the earliest times it was a privileged space, a closed, sanctified world, where the youths and girls met periodically to participate in the mysteries of life and cosmic fecundity. The Taoists took over this archaic cosmological schema—mountain and water— and elaborated it into a richer complex (mountain, water, grotto, trees), but reduced to the smallest scale; it was a paradisal universe in miniature, which was charged with mystical forces because apart from the profane world and in contemplation of which the Taoists sank into meditation.

The sanctity of the closed world is still discernible in the covered bowls of perfumed water symbolizing the sea and the Isles of the Blessed. This complex still served for meditation, just as the miniature gardens did in the beginning, before the fashion for them among scholars in the seventeenth century transformed them into art objects.

Yet it is worth noting that in this example we never witness a complete desacralization of the world, for in the Far East what is called the "esthetic emotion" still retains a religious dimension, even among intellectuals. But the example of the miniature gardens shows us in what direction and by what means the desacralization of the world is accomplished. We need only imagine what an esthetic emotion of this sort could become in a modern society, and we shall understand how the experience of cosmic sanctity can be rarefied and transformed until it becomes a purely human emotion—that, for example, of art for art's sake.

OTHER COSMIC HIEROPHANIES

Considerations of space have obliged us to discuss only a few aspects of the sacrality of nature. Many cosmic hierophanies have necessarily been passed over. Thus, for example, we have not been able to discuss solar and lunar symbols and cults, nor the religious significance of stones, nor the religious role of animals, and so on. Each of these groups of cosmic hierophanies reveals a particular structure of the sacrality of nature; or, more precisely, a modality of the sacred expressed through a specific mode of existence in the cosmos. For example, we need only analyze the various religious values attributed to stones to understand what stones, *as hierophanies*, are able to *show* to man; they reveal power, hardness, permanence. The hierophany of a stone is pre-eminently an ontophany; above all, the stone *is*, it always remains itself, it does not change—and it *strikes* man by what it possesses of irreducibility and absoluteness and, in so doing, reveals to him by analogy the irreducibility and absoluteness of being. Perceived by virtue of a religious experience, the specific mode of existence of the stone reveals to man the nature of an *absolute existence*, beyond time, invulnerable to becoming.[33]

In the same way a rapid analysis of the many and various religious valorizations of the moon shows all that men have deciphered in the lunar rhythms. It is through the moon's phases—that is, its birth, death, and resurrection—that men came to know at once their own mode of being in the cosmos and the chances for their survival or rebirth. It is through lunar symbolism that religious man was led to compare vast masses of apparently unrelated facts and finally to integrate them in a single system. It is even probable that the religious valorization of the lunar rhythms made possible the first great anthropo-cosmic syntheses of the primitives. It was lunar symbolism that enabled man to relate and connect such heterogeneous things as: birth, becoming, death, and resurrection; the waters, plants, woman, fecundity, and immortality; the cosmic darkness, prenatal existence, and life after death, followed by a rebirth of lunar type ("light coming out of darkness"); weaving, the symbol of the "thread of life," fate, temporality, and death; and yet others. In general most of the ideas of cycle, dualism, polarity, opposition, conflict, but also of reconciliation of contraries, of *coincidentia oppositorum*, were either discovered or clarified by virtue of lunar symbolism. We

[33] On sacred stones, cf. Eliade, *Patterns*, pp. 216-238.

may even speak of a metaphysics of the moon, in the sense of a consistent system of "truths" relating to the mode of being peculiar to living creatures, to everything in the cosmos that shares in life, that is, in becoming, growth and waning, death and resurrection. For we must not forget that what the moon reveals to religious man is not only that death is indissolubly linked with life but also, and above all, *that death is not final, that it is always followed by a new birth.*[34]

The moon confers a religious valorization on cosmic becoming and reconciles man to death. The sun, on the contrary, reveals a different mode of existence. The sun does not share in becoming; although always in motion, the sun remains unchangeable; its form is always the same. Solar hierophanies give expression to the religious values of autonomy and power, of sovereignty, of intelligence. This is why, in certain cultures, we witness a process of solarization of the supreme beings. As we saw, the celestial gods tend to disappear from current religion, but in some cases their structure and prestige still survive in the solar gods, especially in the highly developed civilizations that have played an important role in history (Egypt, the Hellenistic East, Mexico).

Many heroic mythologies are solar in structure. The hero is assimilated to the sun; like the sun, he fights darkness, descends into the realm of death and emerges

[34] Cf. *ibid.*, pp. 154-187.

victorious. Here darkness is no longer, as it is in lunar mythologies, one of the modes of being of divinity; instead, it symbolizes all that the god *is not*, hence the adversary *par excellence*. Darkness is no longer valorized as a necessary phase in cosmic life; in the perspective of solar religion, it is opposed to life, to forms, and to intelligence. In some cultures the luminous epiphanies of solar gods become the sign of intelligence. In the end *sun* and *intelligence* will be assimilated to such a degree that the solar and syncretistic theologies of the end of antiquity become rationalistic philosophies; the sun is proclaimed to be the intelligence of the world, and Macrobius sees in the sun all the gods of the Graeco-oriental world, from Apollo and Jupiter to Osiris, Horus, and Adonis (*Saturnalia*, I, ch. 17-23). In the Emperor Julian's treatise *On the Sun King*, as in Proclus' *Hymn to the Sun*, solar hierophanies give place to *ideas*, and religious feeling almost completely disappears after this long process of rationalization.[35]

This desacralization of solar hierophanies is only one among many other similar processes through whose operation the entire cosmos is finally emptied of its religious content. But, as we said, the complete secularization of nature is a fact only for a limited number of moderns—those devoid of all religious feeling. Despite the deep and sweeping changes that Christianity made

[35] Cf. *ibid.*, pp. 124-153.

in the religious valorization of the cosmos and life, it did not reject them. That the whole of cosmic life can still be felt as a cipher of the divinity is shown by a Christian author such as Léon Bloy, when he writes: "Whether life is in men, in animals, or in plants, it is always Life, and when the minute, the inapprehensible point that is called death comes, it is always Jesus who departs, alike from a tree and from a human being."[36]

[36] *Le mendiant ingrat,* II, p. 196.

CHAPTER 4

Human Existence
and Sanctified Life

EXISTENCE OPEN TO THE WORLD

The ultimate aim of the historian of religions is to understand, and to make understandable to others, religious man's behavior and mental universe. It is not always an easy undertaking. For the modern world, religion as form of life and *Weltanschauung* is represented by Christianity. By making a considerable effort, a Western intellectual has at most some chance of familiarizing himself with the religious vision of classical antiquity and even with certain great oriental religions —for example, Hinduism or Confucianism. But such an effort to broaden his religious horizon, praiseworthy though it may be, does not take him far enough; Greece, India, China do not take the Western intellectual beyond the sphere of complex and highly developed religions with a large written sacred literature. To know some part of these sacred literatures, to become familiar with some oriental or classical mythologies and theologies does not yet suffice for a comprehension of the mental universe of *homo religiosus*. These mythologies and theologies are already only too clearly marked by the long labor of scholars; even if, strictly speaking, they are not "religions of the Book" (as are Judaism, Zoroastrianism, Christianity, and Islam), they possess sacred books (India, China) or at least have ben influenced by revered writers of genius (*e.g.*, in Greece, Homer).

To gain a broader religious perspective, it is more useful to become familiar with the folklore of European peoples; in their beliefs and customs, their attitude toward life and death, many archaic religious situations are still recognizable. Studying the rural societies of

Europe provides some basis for understanding the religious world of the neolithic cultivators. In many cases the customs and beliefs of European peasants represent a more archaic state of culture than that documented in the mythology of classic Greece.[1] It is true that most of these rural European populations have been Christianized for over a thousand years. But they succeeded in incorporating into their Christianity a considerable part of their pre-Christian religious heritage, which was of immemorial antiquity. It would be wrong to suppose that for this reason European peasants are not Christians. But we must recognize that their religion is not confined to the historical forms of Christianity, that it still retains a cosmic structure that has been almost entirely lost in the experience of urban Christians. We may speak of a primordial, ahistorical Christianity; becoming Christians, the European cultivators incorporated into their new faith the cosmic religion that they had preserved from prehistoric times.

But for the historian of religions who would understand and make understandable all of the existential situations of *homo religiosus*, the problem is more complex. A whole world stretches beyond the frontiers of the agricultural cultures—the truly "primitive" world of nomadic herdsmen, of totemistic hunters, of peoples still at the stage of gathering and small-game hunting.

[1] This is, for example, the finding of Leopold Schmidt's study, *Gestaltheiligkeit im bäuerlichen Arbeitsmythos*, Vienna, 1952.

To come to know the mental universe of *homo religiosus*, we must above all take into account the men of these primitive societies. Now, to us in this day their culture seems eccentric if not positively aberrant; in any case it is difficult to grasp. But there is no other way of understanding a foreign mental universe than to place oneself *inside* it, at its very center, in order to progress from there to all the values that it possesses.

What we find as soon as we place ourselves in the perspective of religious man of the archaic societies is that *the world exists because it was created by the gods,* and that the existence of the world itself "means" something, "wants to say" something, that the world is neither mute nor opaque, that it is not an inert thing without purpose or significance. For religious man, the cosmos "lives" and "speaks." The mere life of the cosmos is proof of its sanctity, since the cosmos was created by the gods and the gods show themselves to men through cosmic life.

This is why, beginning at a certain stage of culture, man conceives of himself as a microcosm. He forms part of the gods' creation; in other words, he finds in himself the same sanctity that he recognizes in the cosmos. It follows that his life is homologized to cosmic life; as a divine work, the cosmos becomes the paradigmatic image of human existence. To cite a few examples: We have seen that marriage is valorized as a hierogamy of heaven and earth. But among the cultivators, the homology earth-woman is still more complex. Woman is assimilated to the soil, seed to the *semen virile,* and agricultural work to conjugal union. "This woman has come like living soil: sow seed in her, ye men!" says the *Atharva Veda* (XIV, 2, 14). "Your women are as fields for you" (Koran, II, 225). A sterile queen laments, "I am like a field where nothing grows!" On the contrary, in a twelfth-century hymn the Virgin Mary is glorified as "ground not to be plowed, which brought forth fruit" (*terra non arabilis quae fructum parturiit*).

Let us attempt to understand the existential situation of one for whom all these homologies are *experiences* and not simply *ideas.* Clearly, his life has an additional dimension; it is not merely human, it is at the same time cosmic, since it has a transhuman structure. It could be termed an open existence, for it is not strictly confined to man's mode of being. (We know too that the primitive places his model for himself on the transhuman plane revealed by myths). The existence of *homo religiosus,* especially of the primitive, is open to the world; in living, religious man is never alone, part of the world lives in him. But we cannot say, as Hegel did, that primitive man is "buried in nature," that he has not yet found himself as distinct from nature, as himself. The Hindu who, embracing his wife, declares that she is Earth and he Heaven is at the same time fully conscious of his humanity and hers. The Austroasiatic cultivator who uses the same word, *lak,* to designate phallus and spade and, like so many other agriculturalists, assimilates seed to the *semen virile* knows perfectly well that his spade is an instrument that he made and that in tilling his field he performs agricultural work involving knowledge of a certain number of techniques. In other words, cosmic symbolism *adds* a new value to an object or action, without affecting their peculiar and immediate values. An existence open to the world is not an unconscious existence "buried in nature." Openness to the world enables religious man to know himself in knowing the world— and this knowledge is precious to him because it is religious, because it pertains to being.

SANCTIFICATION OF LIFE

The above example helps us to understand the perspective adopted by the man of the archaic societies; for him, the whole of life is capable of being sanctified. The means by which its sanctification is brought about are various, but the result is always the same: life is lived on a twofold plane; it takes its course as human existence and, at the same time, shares in a transhuman life, that of the cosmos or the gods. Probably, in a very distant past, all man's organs and physiological experiences, as well as all his acts, had a religious meaning. This is understandable, for all human behavior was established by the gods or culture heroes *in illo tempore*; they instituted not only the various kinds of work and the various ways of obtaining and eating food, of making love, of expressing thought and feeling, and so on, but even acts apparently of no importance. In the myth of the Australian Karadjeri the two culture heroes took a particular position to urinate, and the Karadjeri still imitate this paradigmatic gesture today.[2] Needless to say, there is nothing corresponding to this on the level of the profane experience of life. For nonreligious man, all vital experiences—whether sex or eating, work or play —have been desacralized. This means that all these physiological acts are deprived of spiritual significance, hence deprived of their truly human dimension.

But aside from this religious meaning that physiological acts receive as imitation of divine models, the organs and their functions were given religious valorization by being assimilated to the various cosmic regions and phenomena. We have already seen a classic example— woman assimilated to the soil and to Mother Earth, the sexual act assimilated to the hierogamy Heaven-Earth and to the sowing of seed. But the number of such homologies established between man and the universe is very large. Some of them seem to force themselves on the mind spontaneously, as, for example, the homology between the eye and the sun, or of the two eyes to sun and moon, or of the cranium to the full moon; or again,

---

[2] Cf. Ralph Piddington, "Karadgeri Initiation," *Oceania*, III, 1932-1933, pp. 46-87.

of breath to the winds, of bones to stones, of hair to grass, and so on.

But the historian of religions encounters other homologies that presuppose a more developed symbolism, a whole system of micro-macrocosmic correspondences. Such, for example, is the assimilation of the belly or the womb to a cave, of the intestines to a labyrinth, of breathing to weaving, of the veins and arteries to the sun and moon, of the backbone to the *axis mundi*, and so on. Of course all these homologies between the human body and the macrocosm are not documented among primitives. Some systems of man-universe correspondences were fully elaborated only in the higher cultures (India, China, the ancient Near East, Central America). Yet their point of departure is already present in archaic cultures. Primitive peoples have revealed to the investigator systems of anthropo-cosmic homologies of extraordinary complexity, which bear witness to an inexhaustible capacity for speculation. Such is the case, for example, with the Dogon in French West Africa.[3]

These anthropo-cosmic homologies concern us particularly in so far as they are ciphers of various existential situations. We said that religious man lives in an open world and that, in addition, his existence is open to the world. This means that religious man is accessible to an infinite series of experiences that could be termed cos-

[3] Cf. Marcel Griaule, *Dieu d'eau. Entretiens avec Ogotemmêli*, Paris, 1948.

mic. Such experiences are always religious, for the world is sacred. If we would understand them, we must remember that the principal physiological functions can become sacraments. Eating is a ritual, and food is variously valorized by various religions and cultures. Foodstuffs are regarded as sacred, or as gifts of divinity, or as an offering to the gods of the body (for example, in India). Sexual life, as we saw, is also ritualized and hence also homologized to divine acts (Heaven-Earth hierogamy). Sometimes marriage is valorized on a threefold plane—individual, social, and cosmic. For example, among the Omahas, the village is divided into two halves, respectively named Heaven and Earth. Marriages can be contracted only between the two exogamic halves, and each new marriage repeats the primordial *hieros gamos*, the union of Heaven and Earth.[4]

Such drawing of anthropo-cosmic homologies and, especially, the sacramentalization of physiological life that ensues have preserved all their vitality even in highly evolved religions. For but one example, we need only think of the prestige that sexual union as ritual acquired in Indian tantrism. India strikingly illustrates how a physiological act can be transformed into ritual and how, when the ritualistic period has ended, the same act can be valorized as mystical technique. The husband's exclamation in the *Brihadāranyaka Upanishad*,

[4] Cf. Werner Müller, *Die blaue Hütte*, Wiesbaden, 1954, pp. 115 ff.

"I am Heaven, thou art Earth," follows the transfiguration of the wife into the Vedic sacrificial altar (VI, 4, 3). But in tantrism woman ends by incarnating Prakriti (= nature) and the cosmic goddess, Shakti, while the male is identified with Shiva, the pure, motionless, serene spirit. Sexual union (*maithuna*) is above all an integration of these two principles, cosmic nature-energy and spirit. As a tantric text expresses it: "The true sexual union is the union of the supreme Shakti with the Spirit (*ātman*); other unions represent only carnal relations with women" (*Kūlārnava Tantra*, V, 111-112). There is no longer any question of a physiological act, there is a mystical rite; the partners are no longer human beings, they are detached and free, like the gods. The tantric texts never tire of emphasizing that a transfiguration of carnal experience occurs. "By the same acts that cause some men to burn in hell for thousands of years, the yogin gains his eternal salvation."[5] The *Brihadāranyaka Upanishad* already declared: "He who knows this, though he seem to commit sin, is pure, clean, ageless, immortal" (V, 14, 8). In other words, "he who knows" has at command an entirely different experience from that of the profane man. This is as much as to say that every human experience is capable of being transfigured, lived on a different, a transhuman plane.

[5] See the texts in Eliade, *Yoga, Immortality and Freedom*, New York, Pantheon Books, Bollingen Series LVI, 1958, pp. 262-263, 411-412. Cited hereafter as *Yoga*.

The Indian example shows to what a degree of mystical refinement sacramentalization of the organs and of physiological life can be brought—a sacramentalization that is already amply documented on all the archaic levels of culture. We should add that the valorization of sexuality as a means of participating in the sacred (or, in India, of gaining the superhuman state of absolute freedom) is not without its dangers. In India itself, tantrism has provided the occasion for aberrant and infamous ceremonies. In the primitive world too, ritual sexuality has been accompanied by many orgiastic forms. Nevertheless, the example still retains its suggestive value, for it reveals an experience that is no longer accessible in a desacralized society—the experience of a sanctified sexual life.

BODY-HOUSE-COSMOS

We have seen that religious man lives in an open cosmos and that he is open to the world. This means (*a*) that he is in communication with the gods; (*b*) that he shares in the sanctity of the world. That religious man can live only in an open world, we saw when we analyzed the structure of sacred space; man desires to dwell at a center, where there is the possibility of communicating with the gods. His dwelling is a microcosm; and so too is his body. The homology house-body-cosmos presents itself very early. We shall dwell on this example a little, for it shows how the values of archaic religious feeling and practice can be reinterpreted by later religions and even philosophies.

Indian religious thought made ample use of this traditional homology, house-cosmos-human body. And the reason is clear: in the last analysis, the body, like the cosmos, is a "situation," a system of conditioning influences that the individual assumes. The spinal column is assimilated to the cosmic pillar (*skambha*) or to Mount Meru; the breaths are identified with the Winds; the navel or heart with the Center of the World, and so on. But homologies are also established between the human body and the entire ritual; the place of sacrifice, the sacrificial utensils and gestures are assimilated to the various physiological functions and organs. The human body, ritually homologized to the cosmos or the Vedic altar (which is an *imago mundi*), is also assimilated to a house. A hatha-yogic text refers to the human body as "a house with a pillar and nine doors" (*Goraksha Shataka*, 14).

All this amounts to saying that by consciously establishing himself in the paradigmatic situation to which he is, as it were, predestined, man cosmicizes himself; in other words, he reproduces on the human scale the system of rhythmic and reciprocal conditioning influences that characterizes and constitutes a world, that, in short, defines any universe. The homology also applies in the reverse direction; in their turn the temple or the

house are regarded as a human body. The "eye" of the
dome is a term that occurs in several architectural traditions.[6] A fact to be emphasized is that each of these
equivalent images—cosmos, house, human body—displays, or is capable of receiving, an upper opening that
makes passage to another world possible. The upper
opening of an Indian tower bears, among other names,
that of *brahmarandhra.* This term designates the opening
at the/top of the skull, which plays a primary role in
yogico-tantric techniques and through which the soul
takes flight at the moment of death. In this connection
we may mention the custom of breaking the skulls of
dead yogins, to facilitate the departure of the soul.[7]

This Indian custom has counterparts in beliefs that
are widely disseminated in Europe and Asia—that the
soul of the dead person departs through the chimney
(= smoke hole) or the roof and especially through the
part of the roof that lies above the "sacred area."[8] In
cases of prolonged death agony, one or more boards are
removed from the roof, or the roof is even broken. The
meaning of this custom is patent: *the soul will more*

[6] Cf. Ananda K. Coomaraswamy, "Symbolism of the Dome," *Indian Historical Quarterly,* XIV, 1938, pp. 34 ff.

[7] Eliade, *Yoga,* p. 423; see also A. K. Coomaraswamy, *loc. cit.,* p. 53,
n. 60.

[8] That part of the sacred space which, in certain types of Eurasiatic
habitations, corresponds to the central post and therefore plays the role
of a Center of the World. See S. G. Ränk, *Die heilige Hinterecke im
Hauskult der Völker Nordosteuropas und Nordasiens,* Helsinki, 1949.

*easily quit its body if the other image of body-cosmos,
the house, is broken open above.* Obviously all these
experiences are inaccessible to nonreligious man, not
only because, for him, death has become desacralized,
but also because he no longer lives in a cosmos in the
proper sense of the word and is no longer aware that
having a body and taking up residence in a house are
equivalent to assuming an existential situation in the
cosmos (see below).

It is noteworthy that the mystical vocabulary of India
has preserved the homology man-house and especially
the assimilation of the skull to the roof or dome. The
fundamental mystical experience—that is, transcending
the human condition—is expressed in a twofold image,
breaking the roof and flight. Buddhistic texts refer to
Arhats who "fly through the air and break the roof of
the palace," who, "flying by their own will, break and
pass through the roof of the house and travel through
the air," and so on.[9] These vivid formulas are capable
of a twofold interpretation: on the plane of mystical
experience there is an "ecstasy" and hence the flight of
the soul through the *brahmarandhra*; on the metaphysical plane there is abolition of the conditioned world.
But both the meanings of the Arhat's flight express a
break in ontological level and passage from one mode
of being to another, or, more precisely, passage from

[9] Cf. Eliade, *Mythes, rêves et mystères*, pp. 133 ff.

conditioned existence to an unconditioned mode of being, that is, to perfect freedom.

In the majority of archaic religions, flight signifies access to a superhuman mode of being (god, magician, spirit)—in the last analysis, freedom to go wherever one will, hence an appropriation of the condition of the spirit. For Indian thought, the Arhat who "breaks the roof of the house" and flies away through the air shows figuratively that he has transcended the cosmos and attained a paradoxical and even inconceivable mode of being, that of absolute freedom (by whatever name it may be called: *nirvāna, asamskrita, samādhi, sahaja,* etc.). On the mythological plane the paradigmatic gesture of transcending the world is illustrated by Buddha proclaiming that he has "broken" the cosmic egg, the "shell of ignorance," and has obtained "the blessed, universal dignity of Buddha."[10]

This example shows the importance of the perennial life of the archaic symbolisms connected with the human habitation. These symbolisms express primordial religious situations, but they are capable of altering their values, can be enriched with new meanings and enter increasingly complex systems of thought. Man inhabits the body in the same way that he inhabits a house or the

[10] *Suttavibhanga,* "Pārājika," I, I, 4, discussed in Paul Mus, "La notion du temps réversible dans la mythologie bouddhique," *Annuaire de l'École pratique des Hautes Études, Section des Sciences Religieuses,* Melun, 1939, p. 13.

cosmos that he has himself created (cf. Chapter 1).
Every lawful and permanent situation implies location
in a cosmos, in a universe perfectly organized and hence
imitated from the paradigmatic model, the Creation.
Inhabited territory, temple, house, body are all, as we
have seen, cosmoses. But each of these cosmoses keeps
an opening, however this idea may be expressed in
different cultures (the eye of the temple, chimney, smoke
hole, *brahmarandhra*, etc.). In one way or another, the
cosmos that one inhabits—body, house, tribal territory,
the whole of this world—communicates above with a
different plane that is transcendent to it.

It can come about that in a noncosmic religion, such
as that of India after Buddhism, the opening to the higher
plane no longer represents passage from the human to
the superhuman condition, but instead expresses transcendence, abolition of the cosmos, absolute freedom.
There is an immense difference between the philosophical meaning of the Buddha's broken egg or the roof
shattered by the Arhats and the archaic symbolism of
passage from earth to heaven along the *axis mundi* or
through the smoke hole. Yet the fact remains that, among
symbols capable of expressing ontological break-
through and transcendence, both Indian philosophy and
Indian mysticism chose this primordial image of shattering the roof. This means that passing beyond the
human condition finds figural expression in the destruction of the "house," that is, of the personal cosmos that

one has chosen to inhabit. Every fixed abode in which one has settled is, on the philosophical plane, equivalent to an existential situation that one has assumed. The image of shattering the roof signifies that one has abolished *all situation*, has rejected settling in the world and chosen absolute freedom, which, for Indian thought, implies annihilation of any conditioned world.

Without entering into any lengthy analysis of the values that one of our nonreligious contemporaries attributes to *his* body, *his* house, and *his* universe, we can already sense the vast distance that separates him from men belonging to the primitive and oriental cultures that we have been discussing. Just as a modern man's habitation has lost its cosmological values, so too his body is without religious or spiritual significance. In a summary formula we might say that for the nonreligious men of the modern age, the cosmos has become opaque, inert, mute; it transmits no message, it holds no cipher. The feeling of the sanctity of nature survives today in Europe chiefly among rural populations, for it is among them that a Christianity lived as a cosmic liturgy still exists.

As for the Christianity of the industrial societies and especially the Christianity of intellectuals, it has long since lost the cosmic values that it still possessed in the Middle Ages. We must add that this does not necessarily imply that urban Christianity is deteriorated or inferior, but only that the religious sense of urban populations is gravely impoverished. The cosmic liturgy, the mystery of nature's participation in the Christological drama, have become inaccessible to Christians living in a modern city. Their religious experience is no longer open to the cosmos. In the last analysis, it is a strictly private experience; salvation is a problem that concerns man and his god; at most, man recognizes that he is responsible not only to God but also to history. But in these man-God-history relationships there is no place for the cosmos. From this it would appear that, even for a genuine Christian, the world is no longer felt as the work of God.

PASSING THROUGH THE NARROW GATE

All that we have just said concerning the body-house symbolism and the anthropo-cosmic homologies that are bound up with it is far from having exhausted the extraordinary richness of the subject; we have had to confine ourselves to only a few of its many aspects. The "house"—since it is at once an *imago mundi* and a replica of the human body—plays a considerable role in rituals and mythologies. In some cultures (*e.g.,* proto-historic China, Etruria, etc.) funerary urns are made in the shape of a house; they have an opening above to permit the dead man's soul to enter and leave.[11] The urn-

---

[11] C. Hentze, *Bronzegerät, Kultbauten, Religion im ältesten China der Chang-Zeit*, Antwerp, 1951, pp. 49 ff.; *id.* in *Sinologica*, III, 1953, pp. 229-239 and Figs. 2-3.

house in some sort becomes the dead man's new "body." But it is also from a house (in this case cap-shaped) that the mythical Ancestor comes; and it is always in such a house-urn-cap that the sun hides at night to come forth again in the morning.[12] Thus there is structural correspondence between the different modes of *passage*—from darkness to light (sun), from a human race's preexistence to its manifestation (mythical Ancestor), from life to death and to the new existence after death (the soul).

We have more than once stressed the fact that all forms of cosmos—universe, temple, house, human body —have an "opening" above. The meaning of this symbolism now becomes still clearer; the opening makes possible *passage* from one mode of being to another, from one existential situation to another. Passage is predestined for every cosmic existence. Man passes from pre-life to life and finally to death, just as the mythical Ancestor passed from pre-existence to existence and the sun passes from darkness to light. We must note that this type of passage is part of a more complex system, the chief characteristics of which we examined in discussing the moon as archetype of cosmic becoming, vegetation as symbol of universal renewal, and especially the many ways of ritually repeating the cosmogony—that is, the paradigmatic *passage* from virtual to formal. All these

[12] C. Hentze, *Tod, Auferstehung, Weltordnung. Das mythische Bild im ältesten China*, Zurich, 1955, pp. 47 ff. and Figs. 24-25.

rituals and symbolisms of passage, we must add, express a particular conception of human existence: when brought to birth, man is not yet completed; he must be born a second time, spiritually; he becomes complete man by passing from an imperfect, embryonic state to a perfect, adult state. In a word, it may be said that human existence attains completion through a series of "passage rites," in short, by successive initiations.

We shall discuss the meaning and function of initiation further on. Here we will dwell for a moment on the symbolism of "passage" as religious man reads it in his familiar surroundings and his daily life—in his house, for example, in the paths that he takes to go to his work, in the bridges he crosses, and so on. This symbolism is present even in the structure of his habitation. As we saw, the upper opening signifies the ascending direction to heaven, the desire for transcendence. The *threshold* concentrates not only the boundary between outside and inside but also the possibility of passage from one zone to another (from the profane to the sacred; cf. Chapter 1). But it is especially the images of the *bridge* and the *narrow gate* which suggest the idea of a dangerous passage and which, for this reason, frequently occur in initiatory and funerary rituals and mythologies. Initiation, death, mystical ecstasy, absolute knowledge, "faith" in Judaeo-Christianity—all these are equivalent to passage from one mode of being to another and bring about a veritable ontological mutation. To suggest this para-

doxical passage (for it always implies a break and a
transcendence), the various religious traditions have
made plentiful use of the symbolism of the Perilous
Bridge or the Narrow Gate. In Iranian mythology the
Cinvat Bridge is traversed by the dead in their *post
mortem* journey; it is nine lance-lengths wide for the
just, but for the wicked it becomes as narrow as "the
blade of a razor" (*Dīnkart*, IX, 20, 3). Under the Cinvat
Bridge lies the mouth of the deep pit of hell (*Vidêvdat*,
3, 7). The mystics always pass over this bridge on their
ecstatic journeys to heaven; over it, for example, passed
the spirit of Ardā Vīrāf.[13]

The *Vision of St. Paul* presents a bridge "narrow as
a hair" connecting our world with Paradise. The same
image is found in Arabic writers and mystics; the bridge
is "narrower than a hair," and links the earth to the astral
spheres and Paradise. Just as in Christian traditions,
sinners cannot cross it and are cast down into hell.
Medieval legends tell of a "bridge under water," and of
the sword bridge which the hero (Lancelot) has to cross
barefoot and with bare hands; it is "sharper than a
scythe" and is crossed in "pain and agony." In Finnish
tradition a bridge covered with needles, nails, and razor
blades crosses hell; the dead, as well as shamans in
ecstasy, use it in their journeys to the other world.
Similar descriptions are found practically all over the

[13] Cf. Eliade, *Le Chamanisme*, pp. 357 ff.

world.[14] But it is important to note that the same imagery
was still used when it became a question of expressing
the difficulty of metaphysical knowledge and, in Christianity, of faith. "A sharpened edge of a razor, hard to
traverse, a difficult path is this—poets declare" (*Katha
Upanishad*, III, 14; tr. Hume, *The Thirteen Principal
Upanishads*, p. 353). "Strait is the gate, and narrow is
the way, which leadeth unto life, and few there be that
find it" (Matthew, 7, 14).

These few examples of the initiatory, funerary, and
metaphysical symbolism of the bridge and the gate have
shown in what way ordinary life and the "little world"
that it implies—the house with its utensils, the daily
routine with its acts and gestures, and so on—can be
valorized on the religious and metaphysical plane. It is
his familiar everyday life that is transfigured in the experience of religious man; he finds a cipher everywhere.
Even the most habitual gesture can signify a spiritual
act. The road and walking can be transfigured into
religious values, for every road can symbolize the "road
of life," and any walk a "pilgrimage," a peregrination
to the Center of the World.[15] If possessing a house implies having assumed a stable situation in the world,
those who have renounced their houses, the pilgrims and
ascetics, proclaim by their "walking," by their constant

---

[14] Cf. *ibid.*, pp. 419 ff.; Maarti Haavio, *Väinämöinen, Eternal Sage*, Helsinki, 1952, pp. 112 ff.
[15] Cf. Eliade, *Patterns*, pp. 430 ff.

movement, their desire to leave the world, their refusal of any worldly situation. The house is a "nest," and, as the *Pañcavimsha Brāhmana* says (XI, 15, 1), the "nest" implies flocks, children, and a "home"; in a word, it symbolizes the world of the family, of society, of getting a living. Those who have chosen the Quest, the road that leads to the Center, must abandon any kind of family and social situation, any "nest," and devote themselves wholly to "walking" toward the supreme truth, which, in highly evolved religions, is synonymous with the Hidden God, the *Deus absconditus.*[16]

RITES OF PASSAGE

It was long ago observed that "rites of passage" play a considerable part in the life of religious man.[17] Certainly, the outstanding passage rite is represented by the puberty initiation, passage from one age group to another (from childhood or adolescence to youth). But there is also a passage rites at birth, at marriage, at death, and it could be said that each of these cases always involves an initiation, for each of them implies a radical change in ontological and social status. When a child is born, he has only a physical existence; he is not yet recognized by his family nor accepted by the community.

[16] Cf. Ananda K. Coomaraswamy, "The Pilgrim's Way," *Journal of the Bihar and Orissa Oriental Research Society*, XXIII, 1937, Part IV, pp. 1-20.

[17] Cf. Arnold van Gennep, *Les rites de passage*, Paris, 1909.

It is the rites performed immediately after birth that give the infant the status of a true "living person"; it is only by virtue of those rites that he is incorporated into the community of the living.

At marriage there is also a passage from one socio-religious group to another. The young husband leaves the group of bachelors and is thenceforth part of the group of heads of families. Every marriage implies a tension and a danger and hence precipitates a crisis; this is why it is performed by a rite of passage. The Greeks called marriage *telos*, consecration, and the marriage ritual resembled that of the mysteries.

In regard to death, the rites are all the more complex because there is not only a "natural phenomenon" (life —or the soul—leaving the body) but also a change in both ontological and social status; the dead person has to undergo certain ordeals that concern his own destiny in the afterlife, but he must also be recognized by the community of the dead and accepted among them. For some peoples, only ritual burial confirms death; he who is not buried according to custom is not dead. Elsewhere a death is not considered valid until after the funerary ceremonies have been performed, or until the soul of the dead person has been ritually conducted to its new dwelling in the other world and there been accepted by the community of the dead. For nonreligious man, birth, marriage, death are events that concern only the individual and his family; or occasionally—in the case of

heads of governments or political leaders—events that
have political repercussions. In a nonreligious view of
life, all these "passages" have lost their ritual character;
that is, they signify no more than is visible in the concrete act of a birth, a death, or an officially recognized
sexual union. However, we must repeat that a drastically
nonreligious experience of the whole of life is seldom
found in the pure state, even in the most secularized
societies. Possibly such a completely nonreligious experience will become commoner in a more or less distant
future; for the present, it is still rare. What is found in
the profane world is a radical secularization of death,
marriage, and birth; but, as we shall soon see, there remain vague memories of abolished religious practices
and even a nostalgia for them.

As for initiatory rituals proper, a distinction must be
made between puberty initiations (age group) and ceremonies for entrance into a secret society. The most important difference lies in the fact that *all* adolescents are
obliged to undergo an age initiation, whereas only a
certain number of adults enter the secret societies. It
seems certain that the institution of puberty initiation is
older than that of the secret society; it is more widely
disseminated and is documented on the most archaic
levels of culture, as, for example, among the Australians
and the Fuegians. We need not here describe initiation
ceremonies in all their complexity. What concerns us is
to show that, even in the archaic stages of culture, initia-

tion plays a leading role in the religious formation of man, and more especially that in essence it consists in a complete change in the novice's ontological status. This fact seems to us of the greatest importance for an understanding of religious man; it shows that the man of the primitive societies does not consider himself "finished" as he finds himself "given" on the natural level of existence. To become a man in the proper sense he must die to this first (natural) life and be reborn to a higher life, which is at once religious and cultural.

In other words, the ideal of humanity that the primitive wishes to attain he sets on a superhuman plane. This means: (1) one does not become a complete man until one has passed beyond, and in some sense abolished, "natural" humanity, for initiation is reducible to a paradoxical, supernatural experience of death and resurrection or of second birth; (2) initiation rites, entailing ordeals and symbolic death and resurrection, were instituted by gods, culture heroes, or mythical ancestors; hence these rites have a superhuman origin, and by performing them the novice imitates a superhuman, divine action. It is important to note this, for it shows once again that religious man *wants to be other* than he finds himself on the "natural" level and undertakes to *make himself* in accordance with the ideal image revealed to him by myths. Primitive man undertakes to attain a *religious ideal of humanity*, and his effort already contains the germs of all the ethics later elaborated in evolved societies. Obviously, in modern nonreligious societies initiation no longer exists as a religious act. But, as we shall see later, the *patterns* of initiation still survive, although markedly desacralized, in the modern world.

PHENOMENOLOGY OF INITIATION

Initiation usually comprises a threefold revelation: revelation of the sacred, of death, and of sexuality.[18] The child knows nothing of these experiences; the initiate knows and assumes them, and incorporates them into his new personality. We must add that, if the novice dies to his infantile, profane, nonregenerate life to be reborn to a new, sanctified existence, he is also reborn to a mode of being that makes learning, *knowledge,* possible. The initiate is not only one newborn or resuscitated; he is a man who *knows,* who has learned the mysteries, who has had revelations that are metaphysical in nature. During his training in the bush he learns the sacred secrets: the myths that tell of the gods and the origin of the world, the true names of the gods, the role and origin of the ritual instruments employed in the initiation ceremonies (the bull-roarers, the flint knives for circumcision, etc.). Initiation is equivalent to a spiritual maturing. And in the religious history of

[18] On the following, see Eliade, *Birth and Rebirth. The Religious Meanings of Initiation in Human Culture,* New York, Harper, 1958.

humanity we constantly find this theme: the initiate, he who has experienced the mysteries, is *he who knows.*

The ceremony everywhere begins with the separation of the candidate from his family and a period of retirement in the bush. Here already there is a symbol of death; the forest, the jungle, darkness symbolize the beyond, the "infernal regions." In some places it is believed that a tiger comes and carries the candidates into the jungle on his back; the feline incarnates the mythical Ancestor, the master of the initiation, who conducts the boys to the underworld. Elsewhere the novice is believed to be swallowed by a monster. In the monster's belly there is cosmic night; it is the embryonic mode of existence, both on the cosmic plane and the plane of human life. In many places there is an initiatory hut in the bush. Here the young candidates undergo part of their ordeals and are instructed in the secret traditions of the tribe. Now, the initiatory hut symbolizes the maternal womb[19]; the novice's symbolic death signifies a regression to the embryonic state. But this is not to be understood only in terms of human physiology but also in cosmological terms; the fetal state is equivalent to a temporary regression to the virtual, precosmic mode.

Other rituals illuminate the symbolism of initiatory death. Among some peoples candidates are buried, or laid in newly dug graves. Or they are covered with

[19] R. Thurnwald, "Primitive Initiations- und Wiedergeburtsriten," *Eranos-Jahrbuch*, VII, 1950, p. 393.

branches and lie motionless like dead men. Or they are daubed with a white powder to make them look like ghosts. In addition, the novices imitate the behavior of ghosts; they do not use their fingers to eat but take food directly with their teeth, as the souls of the dead are believed to do. Finally, the tortures that they undergo—which, of course, have many meanings—have this meaning too: the tormented and mutilated novice is believed to be tortured, cut to pieces, boiled or roasted by the demons who are masters of the initiation, that is, by the mythical ancestors. These physical sufferings correspond to the situation of one who is "eaten" by the feline demon, is cut to pieces in the maw of the initiatory monster, is digested in its belly. The mutilations (knocking out of teeth, amputation of fingers, etc.) also carry a symbolism of death. Most of them are connected with lunar divinities. The moon periodically disappears—that is, dies—to be reborn three nights later. The lunar symbolism emphasizes the conception that death is the preliminary condition for any mystical regeneration.

In addition to specific operations—such as circumcision and subincision—and to initiatory mutilations, other external signs, such as tattooing or scarring, indicate death and resurrection. As for the symbolism of mystical rebirth, it appears in many forms. Candidates are given new names, which will be their true names thenceforth. Among some tribes the young initiates are supposed to have forgotten their former lives completely; immediately after the initiation they are fed like infants, led about by the hand, and reinstructed in all forms of behavior, like babies. Usually they learn a new language in the bush, or at least a secret vocabulary, kept from all but the initiate. It is clear that with initiation everything begins anew. Sometimes the symbolism of the second birth is expressed by concrete gestures. Among some Bantu peoples, before being circumcised the boy is the object of a ceremony called "being born again."[20] His father sacrifices a ram and three days later wraps the boy in the animal's stomach membrane and skin. Just before this is done, the boy must get into bed and cry like an infant. He remains in the ramskin for three days. The same peoples bury their dead in ramskins and in the fetal position. The symbolism of mystical rebirth by ritually donning the skin of an animal is also attested in highly evolved cultures (India, ancient Egypt).

In the scenarios of initiations the symbolism of birth is almost always found side by side with that of death. In initiatory contexts death signifies passing beyond the profane, unsanctified condition, the condition of the "natural man," who is without religious experience, who is blind to spirit. The mystery of initiation gradually reveals to the novice the true dimensions of existence; by introducing him to the sacred, it obliges him to assume

[20] M. Canney, "The Skin of Rebirth," *Man*, No. 91, July 1939, pp. 104-105.

the responsibility that goes with being a man. Here we have a fact of the first importance: for all archaic societies, access to spirituality finds expression in a symbolism of death and a new birth.

MEN'S SOCIETIES AND WOMEN'S SOCIETIES

Rites for entrance into men's societies employ the same ordeals and the same initiatory scenarios. But, as we said, membership in a men's society already implies a choice; not all those who have undergone the puberty initiation will enter the secret society, though they may all wish to.[21]

To cite one example: Among the Mandja and the Banda of Africa, there is a secret society named Ngakola. According to the myth told to the candidates during their initiation, Ngakola was a monster who had the power of swallowing men and then disgorging them renewed. The candidate is put in a hut that symbolizes the monster's body. There he hears Ngakola's eerie voice, there he is whipped and tortured, for he is told that he is now in Ngakola's belly and is being digested. More ordeals follow; then the master of the initiation proclaims that Ngakola, who had devoured the candidate, has disgorged him.[22]

[21] Cf. H. Schurtz, *Altersklassen und Männerbünde*, Berlin, 1902; O. Höfler, *Kultische Geheimbünde der Germanen*, I, Frankfurt-am-Main, 1934; R. Wolfram, *Schwerttanz und Männerbund*, I-III, Kassel, 1936 ff.; W. E. Peuckert, *Geheimkulte*, Heidelberg, 1951.
[22] E. Andersson, *Contribution à l'ethnographie des Kuta*, I, Uppsala, 1953, pp. 264 ff.

This is another instance of the symbolism of death by being swallowed into the belly of a monster, a symbolism that plays so great a role in puberty initiations. We may note again that the rites for entrance into a secret society correspond in every respect to puberty initiations—seclusion, initiatory ordeals and torture, death and resurrection, bestowal of a new name, instruction in a secret language, and so on.

There are also initiations for girls and women. In these feminine rites and mysteries we must not expect to find the same symbolism, or, more precisely, the same symbolic expressions, as those found in men's initiations and confraternities. But it is easy to discern a common element: the foundation for all these rites and mysteries is always a deep religious experience. It is *access to sacrality*, as it is revealed to her who assumes the condition of womanhood, that constitutes the goal both of feminine initiation rites and of women's secret societies.

Initiation begins at the first menstruation. This physiological symptom imposes a break, the girl's forcible removal from her familiar world; she is immediately isolated, separated from the community. The segregation takes place in a special cabin, in the bush, or in a dark corner of the house. The catamenial girl is obliged to remain in a particular and quite uncomfortable position, and must avoid exposing herself to the sun or being touched by anyone. She wears a special dress, or a sign or color allotted to her, and must eat only raw foods.

Segregation and seclusion out of daylight—in a dark

hut, in the bush—suggest the symbolism of the initiatory
death of boys isolated in the forest or shut up in huts.
Yet there is a difference: among girls, segregation occurs
immediately after the first menstruation, hence it is individual; whereas boys are segregated in a group. But
the difference is explained by the fact that in girls the
end of childhood has a physiological manifestation.
However, in the course of time the girls make up a
group, and they are then initiated collectively by old
women who act as their instructors.

As for the women's societies, they are always connected with the mystery of birth and fertility. The mystery of childbearing, that is, woman's discovery that she
is *a creator on the plane of life*, constitutes a religious
experience that cannot be translated into masculine
terms. This makes it clear why childbirth has given rise
to secret feminine rituals, which sometimes attain the
complex organization of real mysteries. Traces of such
mysteries are still preserved even in Europe. [23]

As in the case of men's societies, women's associations
are found in various forms, in which secrecy and mystery progressively increase. To begin, there is the general
initiation that every girl and every young married
woman undergoes; this eventually produces the institution of the women's societies. Next come the women's
mystery associations, as in Africa or, in antiquity, the

[23] Cf. R. Wolfram, "Weiberbünde," *Zeitschrift für Volkskunde,* 42, 1933,
pp. 143 ff.

closed groups of the Maenads. Women's mystery associations of this type were long in disappearing. We need only think of the witches of the Middle Ages and their ritual meetings.

DEATH AND INITIATION

The initiatory symbolism and ritual of being swallowed by a monster has played a considerable role both in initiations and in heroic myths and the mythology of death. The symbolism of return to the ventral cavity always has a cosmological valence. It is the entire world that symbolically returns, with the candidate, into cosmic night, in order that it may be created anew, that is, regenerated. As we saw (Chapter 2), the cosmogonic myth is recited for therapeutic purposes. To be cured, the victim of an illness must be brought to *a second birth*, and the archetypal model of birth is the cosmogony. The work of time must be undone, the auroral moment immediately preceding the Creation must be reintegrated; on the human plane, this is as much as to restore the "blank page" of existence, the absolute beginning, when nothing was yet sullied, nothing spoiled.

Entering the belly of the monster—or being symbolically "buried," or shut up in the initiatory hut—is equivalent to a regression to the primordial nondistinction, to cosmic night. To emerge from the belly or the dark hut or the initiatory "grave" is equivalent to a cosmogony. Initiatory death reiterates the paradigmatic return to chaos, in order to make possible a repetition of the cosmogony—that is, to prepare the new birth. Regression to chaos is sometimes literal—as, for example, in the case of the initiatory sicknesses of future shamans, which have often been regarded as real attacks of insanity. There is, in fact, a total crisis, which sometimes leads to disintegration of the personality.[24] This psychic chaos is the sign that the profane man is undergoing dissolution and that a new personality is on the verge of birth.

We understand why the same initiatory schema—comprising suffering, death, and resurrection (= rebirth)— is found in all mysteries, no less in puberty rites than in the rites for entrance into a secret society, and why the same scenario can be deciphered in the overwhelming inner experiences that precede a mystical vocation (among primitives, the "initiatory sicknesses" of future shamans). Above all, we understand this: the man of the primitive societies has sought to conquer death by transforming it into a *rite of passage*. In other words, for the primitives, men die to something *that was not essential*; men die to the profane life. In short, death comes to be regarded as the supreme initiation, that is, as the beginning of a new spiritual existence. Nor is this all. Generation, death, and regeneration (= rebirth) were under-

[24] Cf. Eliade, *Le Chamanisme*, pp. 36 ff.

stood as three moments in a single mystery, and the entire spiritual effort of archaic man was exerted to show that there must be no intervals between these moments. One cannot *stay* in one of the three. Movement, regeneration continue perpetually. Man constantly reperforms the cosmogony—the paradigmatic making—in order to be sure that he is making something well—a child, for example, or a house, or a spiritual vocation. This is why rites of initiation always present a cosmogonic valence.

"SECOND BIRTH" AND SPIRITUAL GENERATION

The scenario of initiation—death to the profane condition, followed by rebirth to the sacred world, the world of the gods—also plays an important role in highly evolved religions. A celebrated example is the Indian sacrifice. Its purpose is to obtain heaven after death, residence among the gods or the quality of a god (*devātma*). In other words, through the sacrifice the celebrant creates a superhuman condition for himself, a result that may be homologized to that of archaic initiations. Now the sacrificer must first be consecrated by the priests, and this preliminary consecration (*diksha*) carries an initiatory symbolism obstetric in structure; strictly speaking, the *diksha* ritually transforms the sacrificer into an embryo and causes him to be born a second time.

The texts dwell at length on the system of homologies by virtue of which the sacrificer undergoes a "return to the womb," *regressus ad uterum,* followed by a new birth.[25] The relevant passage in the *Aitareya Brāhmana,* for example, runs: "Him whom they consecrate (with the *diksha*) the priests make into an embryo again. With waters they sprinkle; the waters are seed. . . . They conduct him to the hut of the consecrated; the hut of the consecrated is the womb of the consecrated; verily thus they conduct him to his womb. . . . With a garment they cover him; the garment is the caul. . . . Above that is the black antelope skin; the placenta is above the caul. . . . He closes his hands; verily closing its hands the embryo lies within; with closed hands the child is born.[26] . . . Having loosened the black antelope skin, he descends to the final bath; therefore embryos are born freed from the placenta; with the garment he descends; therefore a child is born with a caul" (I, 3; trans. A. B. Keith, *Rigveda Brahmanas,* pp. 108-109).

Sacred knowledge and, by extension, wisdom are conceived as the fruit of an initiation, and it is significant that obstetric symbolism is found connected with the awakening of consciousness both in ancient India and in Greece. Socrates had good reason to compare himself to

[25] Sylvain Lévi, *La doctrine du sacrifice dans les Brāhmanas,* Paris, 1898, pp. 104 ff.; H. Lommel, "Wiedergeburt aus embryonalem Zustand in der Symbolik des altindischen Rituals" in C. Hentze, *Tod, Auferstehung, Weltordnung,* pp. 107-130; Eliade, *Birth and Rebirth,* pp. 53 ff.

[26] On the cosmological symbolism of the closed hand, see C. Hentze, *Tod, Auferstehung, Weltordnung,* pp. 96 ff. and *passim.*

a midwife, for in fact he helped men to be born to consciousness of self; he delivered the "new man." The same symbolism is found in the Buddhist tradition. The monk abandoned his family name and became a "son of the Buddha" (*sakya-putto*), for he was "born among the saints" (*ariya*). So Kassapa said of himself: "Natural Son of the Blessed One, born of his mouth, born of the Dhamma [the Doctrine], fashioned by the Dhamma," etc. (*Samyutta Nikāya*, II, 221, trans. in A. K. Coomaraswamy, "Some Pāli Words," p. 147).

This initiatory birth implied death to profane existence. The schema was maintained in Hinduism as well as in Buddhism. The yogin "dies to this life" in order to be reborn to another mode of being, that represented by liberation. The Buddha taught the way and the means of dying to the profane human condition—that is, to slavery and ignorance—in order to be reborn to the freedom, bliss, and nonconditionality of *nirvāna*. The Indian terminology of initiatory rebirth is sometimes reminiscent of the "new body" that the novice obtains through initiation. The Buddha himself proclaims it: "Moreover, I have shown my disciples the way whereby they call into being out of this body (composed of the four elements) another body of the mind's creation (*rūpim manomayam*), complete in all its limbs and members and with transcendental faculties (*abhinindriyam*)."[27]

---

[27] *Majjhima-Nikāya*, II, 17 (trans. Lord Chalmers, Pt. II, p. 10); cf. also Eliade, *Yoga*, pp. 165 ff.

The symbolism of the second birth or of generation as access to spirituality was adopted and valorized by Alexandrian Judaism and by Christianity. Philo freely uses the theme of generation to refer to birth to a higher life, the life of the spirit (cf., for example, *Abraham*, 20, 99). In his turn, Saint Paul speaks of "spiritual sons," of sons whom he has procreated by faith. "Titus, mine own son after the common faith" (Epistle to Titus, 1, 4). "I beseech thee for my son Onesimus, whom I have begotten in my bonds" (Epistle to Philemon, 10).

There is no need to insist on the differences between the "sons" that Saint Paul "begot" "after the faith" and the "sons of the Buddha" or those whom Socrates "delivered" or the "newborn" of primitive initiations. The differences are obvious. It was the power of the rite itself that "killed" and "resuscitated" the candidate in archaic societies, just as the power of the rite transformed the Hindu sacrificer into an "embryo." The Buddha, on the contrary, "engendered" by his "mouth," that is, by imparting his doctrine (*dhamma*); it was by virtue of the supreme knowledge revealed by the *dhamma* that the disciple was born to a new life that could lead him to the threshold of *nirvāna*. Socrates, for his part, claimed to do no more than exercise the art of the midwife; he helped to "deliver" the true man that each man bore deep within him. For Saint Paul, the situation is different; he engendered "spiritual sons" by the faith, that is, by virtue of a mystery established by Christ.

From one religion to another, from one gnosis or one wisdom to another, the immemorial theme of the second birth is enriched with new values, which sometimes profoundly change the content of the experience. Nevertheless, a common element, an invariable, remains. It could be defined as follows: *access to spiritual life always entails death to the profane condition, followed by a new birth.*

SACRED AND PROFANE IN THE MODERN WORLD

Although we have dwelt on initiation and rites of passage, the subject is far from exhausted; we have done scarcely more than to suggest a few of its essential aspects. And yet, by deciding to discuss initiation at some little length, we have had to pass over a whole series of socio-religious situations that are of considerable interest for an understanding of *homo religiosus.* For example, we have not discussed the sovereign, the shaman, the priest, the warrior, and so on. The fact is that this little book is necessarily summary and incomplete; it represents only a rapid introduction to a vast subject.

It is a vast subject because, as we have said, it concerns not only the historian of religions, the ethnologist, the sociologist, but also the political and social historian, the psychologist, the philosopher. To know the situations assumed by religious man, to understand his spiritual universe, is, in sum, to advance our general knowledge of man. It is true that most of the situations assumed by religious man of the primitive societies and archaic civilizations have long since been left behind by history. But they have not vanished without a trace; they have contributed toward making us what we are today, and so, after all, they form part of our own history.

As we said before, religious man assumes a particular and characteristic mode of existence in the world and, despite the great number of historico-religious forms, this characteristic mode is always recognizable. Whatever the historical context in which he is placed, *homo religiosus* always believes that there is an absolute reality, *the sacred*, which transcends this world but manifests itself in this world, thereby sanctifying it and making it real. He further believes that life has a sacred origin and that human existence realizes all of its potentialities in proportion as it is religious—that is, participates in reality. The gods created man and the world, the culture heroes completed the Creation, and the history of all these divine and semidivine works is preserved in the myths. By reactualizing sacred history, by imitating the divine behavior, man puts and keeps himself close to the gods—that is, in the real and the significant.

It is easy to see all that separates this mode of being in the world from the existence of a nonreligious man. First of all, the nonreligious man refuses transcendence, accepts the relativity of "reality," and may even come to doubt the meaning of existence. The great cultures of the past too have not been entirely without nonreligious men, and it is not impossible that such men existed even on the archaic levels of culture, although as yet no testimony to their existence there has come to light. But it is only in the modern societies of the West that nonreligious man has developed fully. Modern nonreligious man assumes a new existential situation; he regards himself solely as the subject and agent of history, and he refuses all appeal to transcendence. In other words, he accepts no model for humanity outside the human condition as it can be seen in the various historical situations. Man *makes himself*, and he only makes himself completely in proportion as he desacralizes himself and the world. The sacred is the prime obstacle to his freedom. He will become himself only when he is totally demysticized. He will not be truly free until he has killed the last god.

It does not fall to us to discuss this philosophical position. We will only observe that, in the last analysis, modern nonreligious man assumes a tragic existence and that his existential choice is not without its greatness. But this nonreligious man descends from *homo religiosus* and, whether he likes it or not, he is also the work of religious man; his formation begins with the situations assumed by his ancestors. In short, he is the result of a process of desacralization. Just as nature is the product of a progressive secularization of the cosmos as the work of God, profane man is the result of a desacralization of human existence. But this means that nonreligious man has been formed by opposing his predecessor, by attempting to "empty" himself of all religion and all trans-human meaning. He recognizes himself in proportion as he "frees" and "purifies" himself from the "superstitions" of his ancestors. In other words, profane man cannot help preserving some vestiges of the behavior of religious man, though they are emptied of religious meaning. Do what he will, he is an inheritor. He cannot utterly abolish his past, since he is himself the product of his past. He forms himself by a series of denials and refusals, but he continues to be haunted by the realities that he has refused and denied. To acquire a world of his own, he has desacralized the world in which his ancestors lived; but to do so he has been obliged to adopt the opposite of an earlier type of behavior, and that behavior is still emotionally present to him, in one form or another, ready to be reactualized in his deepest being.

For, as we said before, nonreligious man *in the pure state* is a comparatively rare phenomenon, even in the most desacralized of modern societies. The majority of the "irreligious" still behave religiously, even though they are not aware of the fact. We refer not only to the modern man's many "superstitions" and "tabus," all of them magico-religious in structure. But the modern man who feels and claims that he is nonreligious still retains a large stock of camouflaged myths and degenerated rituals. As we remarked earlier, the festivities that go with the New Year or with taking up residence in a new house, although laicized, still exhibit the structure of a ritual of renewal. The same phenomenon is observable in the merrymaking that accompanies a marriage or the birth of a child or obtaining a new position or a social advancement, and so on.

A whole volume could well be written on the myths of modern man, on the mythologies camouflaged in the plays that he enjoys, in the books that he reads. The cinema, that "dream factory," takes over and employs countless mythical motifs—the fight between hero and monster, initiatory combats and ordeals, paradigmatic figures and images (the maiden, the hero, the paradisal landscape, hell, and so on). Even reading includes a mythological function, not only because it replaces the recitation of myths in archaic societies and the oral literature that still lives in the rural communities of Europe, but particularly because, through reading, the modern man succeeds in obtaining an "escape from time" comparable to the "emergence from time" effected by myths. Whether modern man "kills" time with a detective story or enters such a foreign temporal universe as is represented by any novel, reading projects him out of his personal duration and incorporates him into other rhythms, makes him live in another "history."

Strictly speaking, the great majority of the irreligious are not liberated from religious behavior, from theologies and mythologies. They sometimes stagger under a whole magico-religious paraphernalia, which, however, has degenerated to the point of caricature and hence is hard to recognize for what it is. The process of desacralization of human existence has sometimes arrived at hybrid forms of black magic and sheer travesty of religion. We do not refer to the countless "little religions" that proliferate in all modern cities, to the pseudo-occult, neospiritualistic, or so-called hermetic churches, sects, or schools; for all these phenomena still belong to the sphere of religion, even if they almost always present the aberrant aspects of pseudomorphs. Nor do we allude to the various political movements and social utopianisms whose mythological structure and religious fanaticism are visible at a glance. For but one example we need only refer to the mythological structure of communism and its eschatological content. Marx takes over and continues one of the great eschatological myths of the Asiatico-Mediterranean world—the redeeming role of the Just (the "chosen," the "anointed," the "innocent," the "messenger"; in our day, the proletariat), whose sufferings are destined to change the ontological status of the world. In fact, Marx's classless society and the consequent disappearance of historical tensions find their closest precedent in the myth of the Golden Age that many traditions put at the beginning and the end of history. Marx enriched this venerable myth by a whole Judaeo-Christian messianic ideology: on the one hand, the prophetic role and soteriological function that he attributes to the proletariat; on the other, the final battle between Good and Evil, which is easily comparable to the apocalyptic battle between Christ and Antichrist, followed by the total victory of the former. It is even significant that Marx takes over for his own purposes the Judaeo-Christian eschatological hope of *an absolute end to history*; in this he differs from other historicistic philosophers (Croce and Ortega y Gasset, for example), for whom the tensions of history are consubstantial with the human condition and therefore can never be completely done away with.

But it is not only in the "little religions" or in the political mystiques that we find degenerated or camouflaged religious behavior. It is no less to be seen in movements that openly avow themselves to be secular or even antireligious. Examples are nudism or the movements for complete sexual freedom, ideologies in which we can discern traces of the "nostalgia for Eden," the desire to re-establish the paradisal state before the Fall, when sin did not yet exist and there was no conflict between the pleasures of the flesh and conscience.

Then, too, it is interesting to observe to what an extent the scenarios of initiation still persist in many of the acts and gestures of contemporary nonreligious man. We shall, of course, disregard the situations in which a certain type of initiation survives in degenerate form. A good example is war, and especially individual combats (particularly between aviators)—exploits that involve "ordeals" that can be homologized to those of traditional military initiations, even if in our day the combatants are no longer aware of the deeper significance of their "ordeals" and hence scarcely benefit by their initiatory meaning. But even specifically modern techniques, such as psychoanalysis, still preserve the initiatory pattern. The patient is asked to descend deeply into himself, to make his past live, to confront his traumatic experiences again; and, from the point of view of form, this dangerous operation resembles initiatory descents into hell, the realm of ghosts, and combats with monsters. Just as the initiate was expected to emerge from his ordeals victorious—in short, was to "die" and be "resuscitated" in order to gain access to a fully responsible existence, open to spiritual values—so the patient undergoing analysis today must confront his own "unconscious," haunted by ghosts and monsters, in order to find psychic health and integrity and hence the world of cultural values.

But initiation is so closely linked to the mode of being of human existence that a considerable number of modern man's acts and gestures continue to repeat initiatory scenarios. Very often the "struggle for life," the "ordeals" and "difficulties" that stand in the way of a vocation or a career, in some sort reiterate the ordeals of initiation; it is after the "blows" that are dealt him, the moral and even physical "suffering" and "torture" he undergoes, that a young man "proves" himself, knows his possibilities, grows conscious of his powers, and finally becomes himself, spiritually adult and creative (the spirituality is, of course, what is understood as such in the modern world). For every human existence is formed by a series of ordeals, by repeated experience of "death" and "resurrection." And this is why, in a religious perspective, existence is established by initiation; it could almost be said that, in so far as human existence is fulfilled, it is itself an initiation.

In short, the majority of men "without religion" still hold to pseudo religions and degenerated mythologies. There is nothing surprising in this, for, as we saw, profane man is the descendant of *homo religiosus* and he cannot wipe out his own history—that is, the behavior of his religious ancestors which has made him what he is today. This is all the more true because a great part of his existence is fed by impulses that come to him from the depths of his being, from the zone that has been called the "unconscious." A purely rational man is an abstraction; he is never found in real life. Every human being is made up at once of his conscious activity and his irrational experiences. Now, the contents and structures of the unconscious exhibit astonishing similarities to mythological images and figures. We do not mean to say that mythologies are the "product" of the unconscious, for the mode of being of the myth is precisely that *it reveals itself as myth*, that is, it announces that something *has been manifested in a paradigmatic man-ner.* A myth is "produced" by the unconscious in the same sense in which we could say that *Madame Bovary* is the "product" of an adultery.

Yet the contents and structures of the unconscious are the result of immemorial existential situations, especially of critical situations, and this is why the unconscious has a religious aura. For every existential crisis once again puts in question both the reality of the world and man's presence in the world. This means that the existential crisis is, finally, "religious," since on the archaic levels of culture *being* and *the sacred* are one. As we saw, it is the experience of the sacred that founds the world, and even the most elementary religion is, above all, an ontology. In other words, in so far as the unconscious is the result of countless existential experiences, it cannot but resemble the various religious universes. For religion is the paradigmatic solution for every existential crisis. It is the paradigmatic solution not only because it can be indefinitely repeated, but also because it is believed to have a transcendental origin and hence is valorized as a revelation received from an *other,* transhuman world. The religious solution not only resolves the crisis but at the same time makes existence "open" to values that are no longer contingent or particular, thus enabling man to transcend personal situations and, finally, gain access to the world of spirit.

This is not the place to develop all the consequences

of this close relation between the content and structures of the unconscious on the one hand and the values of religion on the other. We were led to refer to it in order to show in what sense even the most avowedly nonreligious man still, in his deeper being, shares in a religiously oriented behavior. But modern man's "private mythologies"—his dreams, reveries, fantasies, and so on—never rise to the ontological status of myths, precisely because they are not experienced by the *whole man* and therefore do not transform a particular situation into a situation that is paradigmatic. In the same way, modern man's anxieties, his experiences in dream or imagination, although "religious" from the point of view of form, do not, as in *homo religiosus*, make part of a *Weltanschauung* and provide the basis for a system of behavior. An example will show the differences between these two categories of experiences. The unconscious activity of modern man ceaselessly presents him with innumerable symbols, and each of them has a particular message to transmit, a particular mission to accomplish, in order to ensure or to re-establish the equilibrium of the psyche. As we have seen, the symbol not only makes the world "open" but also helps religious man to attain to the universal. For it is through symbols that man finds his way out of his particular situation and "opens himself" to the general and the universal. Symbols awaken individual experience and transmute it into a spiritual act, into metaphysical comprehension of the world. In the presence of any tree, symbol of the world tree and image of cosmic life, a man of the premodern societies can attain to the highest spirituality, for, by understanding the symbol, *he succeeds in living the universal*. It is the religious vision of the world, and the concomitant ideology, that enable him to make this individual experience bear fruit, to "open" it to the universal. The image of the tree still quite frequently appears in the imaginary universes of modern nonreligious man; it is a cipher of his deeper life, of the drama that is played out in his unconscious and that concerns the integrity of his psychomental life and hence his own existence. But as long as the symbol of the tree does not awaken his total consciousness and "open" it to the universe, it cannot be said to have completely fulfilled its function. It has only partly "saved" him from his individual situation—for example, by enabling him to resolve a deep crisis and restoring his temporarily threatened psychic equilibrium; but it has not yet raised him to spirituality—that is, it has not succeeded in revealing one of the structures of the real to him.

This example, it seems to us, suffices to show in what way the nonreligious man of modern societies is still nourished and aided by the activity of his unconscious, yet without thereby attaining to a properly religious experience and vision of the world. The unconscious offers him solutions for the difficulties of his own life, and in this way plays the role of religion, for, before making an existence a creator of values, religion ensures its integrity. From one point of view it could almost be said that in the case of those moderns who proclaim that they are nonreligious, religion and mythology are "eclipsed" in the darkness of their unconscious—which means too that in such men the possibility of reintegrating a religious vision of life lies at a great depth. Or, from the Christian point of view, it could also be said that nonreligion is equivalent to a new "fall" of man— in other words, that nonreligious man has lost the capacity to live religion consciously, and hence to understand and assume it; but that, in his deepest being, he still retains a memory of it, as, after the first "fall," his ancestor, the primordial man, retained intelligence enough to enable him to rediscover the traces of God that are visible in the world. After the first "fall," the religious sense descended to the level of the "divided" consciousness"; now, after the second, it has fallen even further, into the depths of the unconscious; it has been "forgotten."

Here the considerations of the historian of religions end. Here begins the realm of problems proper to the philosopher, the psychologist, and even the theologian.

**CHRONOLOGICAL
SURVEY**

The "History of Religion" as a Branch of Knowledge

The science of religions, as an autonomous discipline devoted to analyzing the common elements of the different religions and seeking to deduce the laws of their evolution, and especially to discover and define the origin and first form of religion, is a very recent addition to the sciences. It dates from the nineteenth century and was founded at almost the same time as the science of language. Max Müller gave it the name "science of religions" or "comparative study of religions" in the Preface to the first volume of his *Chips from a German Workshop* (London, 1867). It is true that the term "science of religions" had been sporadically used earlier (in 1852 by the Abbé Prosper Leblanc, in 1858 by Stiefelhagen, etc.), but not in the strict sense given it by Max Müller, which then passed into current usage.

The first university chair of the History of Religions was founded at Geneva in 1873; in 1876, four were established in Holland. In 1879 a chair was instituted at the Collège de France, and in 1885 a special Section of Religious Sciences was organized at the École des Hautes Études at the Sorbonne. The Free University of Brussels instituted a chair of the History of Religions in 1884. Germany followed in 1910, with the first chair at Berlin and others later at Leipzig and Bonn. The other European countries fell in with the trend.

In 1880 the *Revue de l'Histoire des Religions* was founded at Paris by M. Vernes; in 1898 the *Archiv für Religionswissenschaft* at Freiburg-im-Breisgau by Dr. Achelis; in 1905 *Anthropos*, a journal devoted chiefly to primitive religions, at St. Gabriel-Mödling, near Vienna, by Wilhelm Schmidt; in 1925 *Studi e Materiali di Storia delle Religioni*, by R. Pettazoni. American journals in the field are *The Journal of Religion* (University of Chicago, from 1921) and *The Review of Religion* (Columbia University, from 1936). In Germany the place of the *Archiv für Religionswissenschaft*, which ceased publication after the end of the Second World War, has been taken by the *Zeitschrift für Religions- und Geistesgeschichte* (from 1948). *Zalmoxis: Revue des Études Religieuses*, founded by Mircea Eliade in 1938, ceased publication after its third volume (Paris-Bucharest, 1938-1942). *Numen, International Review for the History of Religions*, issued by the International Association for the History of Religions and edited by R. Pettazoni, has been published at Leiden since 1954. The same association has brought out the *International Bibliography of the History of Religions*, for the years 1952 ff. (published since 1954).

The First International Congress for the Sciences of Religion was held in 1897, at Stockholm. In 1900 the Congrès d'Histoire des Religions opened at Paris; its name was intended to exclude theology and the so-called philosophy of religion from its deliberations. The Ninth International Congress was held at Tokyo in 1958.

Gradually bibliographies, dictionaries, encyclopedias multiplied; publication of sources also increased. Particularly noteworthy are *Encyclopaedia of Religion and Ethics* (13 vols., Edinburgh, 1908-1923), edited by J.

Hastings; *Die Religion in Geschichte und Gegenwart. Handwörterbuch für Theologie und Religionswissenschaft* (5 vols., Tübingen, 1909-1913; a third edition is in course of publication); *Religionsgeschichtliche Lesebuch*, edited by A. Bertholet (Tübingen, 1908 ff.; 2nd ed., 1926 ff.); *Textbuch zur Religionsgeschichte*, edited by E. Lehmann (Leipzig, 1912), later by E. Lehmann and H. Haas; *Fontes historiae religionum ex auctoribus graecis et latinis*, edited by C. Clemen (Bonn, 1920 ff.); H. Haas (and others), *Bilderatlas zur Religionsgeschichte* (Leipzig, 1924 ff.); J. B. Pritchard, *Ancient Near Eastern Texts relating to the Old Testament* (Princeton, 1950), and *The Ancient Near East in Pictures relating to the Old Testament* (Princeton, 1954).

But though the science of religions as an autonomous discipline had its beginning only in the nineteenth century, interest in the history of religions goes back much further into the past. (On the following, see H. Pinard de la Boullaye, *L'étude comparée des religions*, Paris, 1922, 2 vols., third edition revised and corrected, 1929; Gustav Mensching, *Geschichte der Religionswissenschaft*, Bonn, 1948.) We find it documented for the first time in classic Greece, particularly from the fifth century. The interest was manifested in two ways: by travelers' accounts that included descriptions of foreign cults and comparisons with Greek religious practices, and by philosophic criticism of the traditional religion. Herodotus (*c.* 484-*c.* 425 B.C.) already presented surprisingly

accurate descriptions of several barbarian and exotic
religions (Egypt, Persia, Thrace, Scythia, etc.) and even
advanced hypotheses concerning their origin and their
relations to the cults and mythologies of Greece. The
pre-Socratic thinkers inquired into the nature of the gods
and the value of myths and founded rationalistic criticism
of religion. Thus, for example, for Parmenides (born
c. 520) and Empedocles (*c.* 495-435) the gods were
personifications of natural forces. Democritus (*c.* 460-
370) even seems to have been curiously interested in
foreign religions, which he knew at the source from his
numerous journeys; a book on the *Sacred Writings of
Babylon* was attributed to him, as well as a *Chaldean
Treatise* and a *Phrygian Treatise*. Plato (429-347) made
frequent use of comparisons with the religions of the
barbarians. As for Aristotle (384-322), he first sys-
tematically formulated the theory of the religious degeneration of humanity (*Metaphysics*, XII, ch. 7), an idea
that would often be revived in later times. Theophrastus
(372-287), who succeeded Aristotle as head of the
Lyceum, may be considered the first Greek historian of
religions; according to Diogenes Laertius (V, 48), he
composed a history of religions in six books.

But it was especially after the conquests of Alexander
the Great (356-323) that Greek writers had the opportunity to obtain direct knowledge of the religious traditions of the oriental peoples and to describe them. Under
Alexander, Berosus, a priest of Bel, published his *Baby-*

loniaca. Megasthenes who, between 302 and 297, was
several times sent as ambassador to the Indian King
Sandrakottos (= Chandragupta) by Seleucus Nicator,
published his *Indica.* Hecataeus of Abdera or Teos (365-
270/275) wrote on the Hyperboreans and devoted his
Aegyptica to the theology of the Egyptians. Manetho
(3rd century), an Egyptian priest, dealt with the same
subject in a work published under the same title. The
Alexandrian world thus came to know a considerable
number of exotic myths, rites, and religious customs.

At Athens in the beginning of the third century,
Epicurus (341-270) undertook a radical criticism of
religion; in his view, the "universal consensus" proves
that the gods exist, but he regards them as superior and
distant beings who have no relation to man. His theses
became especially popular in the Latin world of the first
century B.C., due largely to the genius of Lucretius
(*c.* 98-*c.* 53).

But it was the Stoics who deeply influenced the whole
of late antiquity by developing the method of allegorical
interpretation, which enabled them to preserve and at
the same time to revalorize the mythological heritage.
According to the Stoics, myths reveal either philosophical views on the basic nature of things or ethical doctrines. The many names of the gods designate one sole
divinity, and all religions express the same fundamental
truth—only the terminology varies. The Stoic allegorical
method made it possible to translate any ancient or

exotic tradition into a universal and easily understandable language. The method gained wide acceptance, and it was frequently employed later.

The idea that some gods were kings or heroes deified for the services that they had rendered to humanity had found proponents from the time of Herodotus. But it was Euhemerus (*c.* 330-*c.* 260) who popularized this pseudohistorical interpretation of mythology in his treatise *The Sacred Scripture*. Euhemerism found many adherents, due chiefly to the fact that the poet Ennius (239-169) translated *The Sacred Scripture* into Latin and that the Christian polemicists later took over Euhemerus's arguments. Proceeding with a far stricter historical method, the historian Polybius (*c.* 210/205-*c.* 125) and the geographer Strabo (*c.* 60-*c.* A.D. 25) attempted to discover the possible historical elements in certain myths.

Among the Roman eclectics, Cicero (106-43) and Varro (116-27) deserve particular mention for the historico-religious value of their work. The forty books of Varro's *Roman Antiquities* were a storehouse of erudition. In his *On the Nature of the Gods*, Cicero gave a quite accurate description of the state of rites and beliefs in the last century of the pagan era.

The spread of oriental cults and mystery religions in the Roman Empire and the religious syncretism that resulted, especially in Alexandria, were favorable to a knowledge of exotic religions and to study of the religious antiquities of various countries. During the first two centuries of the Christian era, the euhemerist Herennius Philon published his *Phoenician History*, Pausanias his *Description of Greece*—an inexhaustible mine for the historian of religions—and the pseudo Apollodorus his *Library*, a work on mythology. Neo-Pythagoreanism and Neo-Platonism applied themselves to revalorizing the spiritual interpretation of myths and rites. A typical representative of this school of exegesis is Plutarch (45/50-c. 125), especially in his treatise *On Isis and Osiris*. In his view the diversity of religious forms was only apparent; symbols revealed the fundamental unity of religions. The Stoic thesis was brilliantly restated by Seneca (2-66): the many divinities were aspects of one God. Meanwhile descriptions of foreign religions and esoteric cults multiplied. Julius Caesar (104-44 B.C.) and Tacitus (ca. 55-120) furnished valuable information concerning the religions of the Gauls and the Germans; Apuleius (2nd century A.D.) described the ceremony of initiation into the mysteries of Isis; Lucian gave an account of the Syrian cult in his *On the Syrian Goddess* (c. A.D. 120).

For the Christian apologists and heresiarchs, the problem presented itself on a different plane, for they opposed the one God of the revealed religion to the many gods of Paganism. Hence they were compelled, on the one hand, to demonstrate the supernatural origin and consequent superiority of Christianity, and, on the other, to account for the origin of the pagan gods and especially

to explain why the pre-Christian world had been idola-
trous. They also had to explain the resemblances between
the mystery religions and Christianity. Several theses
were advanced: (1) the demons, born from intercourse
between the fallen angels and the "daughters of men"
(Genesis, 6, 2), had driven mankind to idolatry; (2)
plagiarism (the evil angels, knowing the prophecies, had
introduced certain resemblances to Judaism and Christianity into the pagan religions, to trouble believers; the
pagan philosophers had borrowed their doctrines from
Moses and the Prophets); (4) human reason can attain
to knowledge of truth by its own power, hence the pagan
world could have a natural knowledge of God.

The pagan reaction took various forms. It is manifested by the violent attack (*c.* 178) of the Neo-Pytha-
gorean Celsus on the originality and spiritual value of
Christianity; by the *Life of Apollonius of Tyana* (by the
sophist Philostratus, *c.* 175-*c.* 249), in which the religious conceptions of the Indians, Greeks, and Egyptians
are compared and which expounds a pagan ideal of
piety and tolerance; by the Neo-Platonist Porphyry
(*c.* 233-*c.* 305), disciple and editor of Plotinus, who
skillfully attacks Christianity by employing the allegorical method; by Iamblichus (*c.* 280-*c.* 330), who urges
an ideal of syncretism and tolerance.

The outstanding figures in the Christian counterattack
were the Africans Minucius Felix, Lactantius, Tertullian,
and Firmicius Maternus, and the great Alexandrian

scholars Clement of Alexandria and Origen. Eusebius
of Caesarea in his *Chronicle*, Saint Augustine in the *City
of God*, and Paulus Orosius in his *Histories* dealt out
the last refutations to paganism. They agree with the
pagan writers in maintaining the thesis of the increasing
degeneration of religions. Their writings, like those of
their opponents and of other Christian authors, have
preserved much historico-religious material in regard
to the myths, rites, and customs of nearly all the peoples
of the Roman Empire as well as to the Gnostics and
the heretical Christian sects.

Interest in foreign religions was awakened in the West
during the Middle Ages by the threatening presence of
Islam. In 1141 Peter the Venerable had the *Koran*
translated by Robert de Rétines, and schools for the
study of Arabic were founded in 1250. By that date,
Islam had already produced important works on the
subject of pagan religions. Al-Bīrunī (973-1048) had
given a remarkable description of Indian religions and
philosophies; Shahrastānī (d. 1153) was the author of
a treatise on the Islamic schools; Ibn Hazm (994-1064)
had compiled a voluminous and erudite *Book of Decisive
Solutions concerning Religions, Sects, and Schools*, in
which he discussed Mazdean and Manichaean dualism,
Brahmans, Jews, Christians, atheists, and several Islamic
sects. But it was especially Averroes (ibn-Rushd, 1126-
1198) who, after profoundly influencing Islamic thinking, was destined to give the first impulse to a whole

intellectual trend in the West. In interpreting religion, Averroes employed the symbolical and allegorical method. He concluded that all the monotheistic religions were true, but he shared Aristotle's opinion that, in an eternal world, religions appear and disappear again and again.

Among the Jewish scholars of the Middle Ages, two demand particular mention: Saadia (892-942), in his *Book of Beliefs and Convictions* (c. 933), expounded the religions of the Brahmans, the Christians, and the Muslims in the framework of a religious philosophy. Maimonides (1135-1204) undertook a comparative study of religions, scrupulously avoiding the syncretistic position. He attempted to explain the imperfections of the first revealed religion, Judaism, by the doctrine of divine condescension and human progress, theses that had also been advanced by the Fathers of the Church.

The appearance of the Mongols in Asia Minor and their hostility to the Arabs led the Popes to send missions to inquire into their religions and customs. In 1244 Innocent IV despatched two Dominicans and two Franciscans, one of whom, Jean du Plan de Carpin, made his way as far as Karakorum, in Central Asia, and on his return wrote his *History of the Mongols*. In 1253 Louis IX sent William Ruysbroek to Karakorum, where, he tells us, he withstood the Manichaeans and Saracens in debate. Finally, in 1274, the Venetian Marco Polo published his *Book,* in which, among countless other oriental wonders, he told of the life of the Buddha. All these books were immensely successful. On the basis of this new documentation, Vincent of Beauvals, Roger Bacon, and Raymond Lully expounded the beliefs of the "idolaters," Tartars, Jews, and Saracens in various works. The theses of the earliest Christian apologists were taken up again—notably the doctrine of spontaneous knowledge of God and the theses of degeneration and of demonic influence in the spread of polytheism.

The Renaissance rediscovered and revalorized paganism, primarily because of the fashion for Neo-Platonic allegorical interpretation. Marsilio Ficino (1433-1499) edited Porphyry, the pseudo Iamblichus, and Hermes Trismegistus, and composed a *Platonic Theology*; he considered Plotinus' last disciples to be the most authoritative interpreters of Plato. The Humanists believed that there was a tradition common to all religions, that knowledge of it sufficed for salvation, and that in the last analysis all religions were equal in value. The year 1520 saw the appearance of the first general history of religions: *The Customs, Laws, and Rites of all Peoples*, by Jean Boem, of the Teutonic Order; it contained descriptions of African, Asian, and European beliefs.

The geographical discoveries of the fifteenth and sixteeth centuries opened new horizons for a knowledge of religious man. The narratives of the first explorers were brought together in collections of *Voyages* and had an enormous vogue among the educated European public.

They were followed by the *Letters* and *Relations* published by missionaries to America and China. A first attempt to compare the religions of the New World with those of antiquity was made by the missionary J. F. Lafitau in his *Customs of the American Savages compared to the Customs of the Earliest Ages*, published at Paris in 1724. In 1757 Charles De Brosses produced an essay *On the Cult of Fetish Gods, or Parallel between the Ancient Egyptian Religion and the Present Religion of Nigritia* and presented it to the French Academy of Inscriptions, but the Academy considered it too daring to publish and it appeared anonymously in 1760. Answering Lafitau and following Hume, De Brosses maintained that it was an error to believe that mankind had first possessed a pure idea of God, which later degenerated; on the contrary, "since the human mind rises by degrees from the lower to the higher," the first form of religion could only have been crude, that is, "fetishism," a term that De Brosses used in the vague sense of the cult of animals, plants, and inanimate objects.

The English Deists, especially Hume, the French "philosophers" and encyclopedists—Rousseau, Voltaire, Diderot, d'Alembert—and the Germans of the Enlightenment (particularly F. A. Wolf and Lessing) vigorously continued the discussion of the problem of natural religion. But it was the scholarly investigators who made a positive contribution to the interpretation of exotic, pagan, or primitive religions. Certain authors exercised a great influence, both by the hypotheses that they advanced and by the reactions that their works produced. Fontenelle, in his *Discourse on the Origin of Fables* (published in 1724, but composed between 1680 and 1699), exhibited a penetrating historical sense and anticipated the animistic theories of the nineteenth century. In 1794 François Dupuis published *The Origin of all Cults*, in which he sought to show that the history of the gods, and even the life of Christ, are only allegories of the motions of the stars, a thesis that was revived by the Pan-Babylonians at the end of the nineteenth century. Friedrich Creuzer, in his *Symbolism and Mythology of Ancient Peoples, especially the Greeks* (1810-1812), attempted to reconstruct the primordial phases of "Pelasgian" and oriental religions, and to show the role of symbols. (His theses were demolished by the rationalist Christian August Lobeck, in an immense work published in 1829, *Aglaophamus*.)

As a result of the discoveries made in all branches of oriental studies during the first half of the nineteenth century, as well as of the establishment of Indo-European philology and comparative linguistics, the history of religions first really entered into its own with Max Müller (1823-1900). His *Essay on Comparative Mythology* (1856) is the first of a long series of studies by himself and the disciples of his theory. Max Müller found the genesis of myths in natural phenomena, especially in solar epiphanies, and explained the birth of the gods as a "disease of language"—what had originally been but a name, *nomen*, became a divinity, *numen*. His theses met with considerable success and lost their popularity only toward the end of the nineteenth century, as the result of the work of W. Mannhardt (1831-1880) and of Edward Burnett Tylor (1832-1917). In his principal book, *Cults of Forest and Field* (1875-77), Mannhardt showed the importance of the "lower mythology" still surviving in the rites and beliefs of peasants; in his view, these beliefs represented an earlier stage of religion than the naturalistic mythologies studied by Max Müller. Mannhardt's theses were adopted and popularized by Sir James George Frazer in *The Golden Bough* (1890; 3rd ed. 1907-1913, twelve volumes). In 1871 appeared E. B. Tylor's *Primitive Culture*, which was epoch-making in that it launched a new vogue, that of animism. According to Tylor's animistic theory, primitive man believed that everything was endowed with a soul, and this fundamental and universal belief explained not only the cult of the dead and of ancestors but also the genesis of the gods. A new theory, that of pre-animism, was developed from 1900 by R. R. Marrett, K. T. Preuss, and other scholars. According to this theory the origin of religion was to be sought in the experience of an impersonal force (*mana*). A critique of animism, but from a different point of view, was advanced by Andrew Lang (1844-1912); he had observed the belief in supreme beings ("All Fathers") on archaic levels of culture, and could not explain it by a belief in spirits. Wilhelm Schmidt (1868-1954) took up this idea and, developing it from the standpoint of the methodology of "cultural history" (*Kulturgeschichte*), attempted to demonstrate the existence of a primordial monotheism (cf. *Der Ursprung der Gottesidee* [The Origin of the Idea of God], 12 vols., 1912-1955).

Other movements appeared toward the end of the nineteenth century and the beginning of the twentieth. Emile Durkheim (1858-1917) believed that he had found the sociological explanation for religion in totemism. (Among the Ojibwa Indians of North America the term *totem* designates the animal whose name a clan bears and which is regarded as their ancestor.) As early as 1869, J. F. MacLennan had asserted that totemism represented the original form of religion. But later investigations, especially the work of Frazer, showed that totemism is not universally disseminated and that it cannot be regarded as the earliest form taken by religion. Lucien Lévy-Bruhl sought to prove that religious behavior could be explained by the prelogical mentality of primitives—a hypothesis that he renounced toward the end of his life. But these sociological hypotheses had no lasting influence on historico-religious studies. A certain number of ethnologists attempted to approach their science as a historical discipline, and their studies indirectly made an important contribution to the history of religions. Among these historically oriented ethnologists, we may cite: F. Graebner, Leo Frobenius, W. W. Rivers, and Wilhelm Schmidt in Europe, and Franz Boas and his school in America. Psychological explanations for religion were proposed by Wilhelm Wundt (1832-1920), William James (1842-1910), and Sigmund Freud (1856-1939). The phenomenology of religion had its first authoritative representative in Gerardus van der Leeuw (1890-1950).

At present, historians of religions are divided between two divergent but complementary methodological orientations. One group concentrate primarily on the characteristic *structures* of religious phenomena, the other choose to investigate their *historical context*. The former seek to understand the *essence of religion*, the latter to discover and communicate its *history*.

**BIBLIOGRAPHY
AND INDEX**

Selected

Bibliography

INTRODUCTION

Caillois, R., *L'homme et le sacré*, 2nd ed., Paris, 1953

Chantepie de la Saussaye, P. D., *Lehrbuch der Religions-geschichte*, 4th ed., rev. A. Bertholet and E. Lehmann, 2 vols., Tübingen, 1924-1925

Clemen, C., *et al.*, *Die Religionen der Erde*, Munich, 1927
————, *Urgeschichtliche Religion. Die Religionen der Stein-, Bronze- und Eisenzeit*, I-II, Bonn, 1932-1933

Durkheim, E., *Les formes élémentaires de la vie religieuse*, Paris, 1912

Eliade, M., *Traité d'histoire des religions*, Paris, 1949 (= *Patterns in Comparative Religion*, New York, 1958)

Firth, R., "The Analysis of Mana: An Empirical Approach," *The Journal of the Polynesian Society*, 49, 1940, pp. 483-510

Gorce, M., R. Mortier, *et al.*, *Histoire générale des religions*, I-V, Paris, 1944-1951

Haekel, J., "Zum heutigen Forschungsstand der historischen Ethnologie," *Wiener Schule der Völkerkunde*, Vienna, 1955

König, F., *et al., Christus und die Religionen der Erde*, I-III, Freiburg im Breisgau, 1951

Koppers, W., *Urmensch und Urreligion*, Olten, 1944; 2nd ed., 1946. (*Primitive Man and His World Picture*, London, 1925)

——, "Ethnologie und Geschichte," *Anthropos*, 50, 1955, pp. 943-948

Leeuw, G. van der, *Phänomenologie der Religion*, Tübingen, 1933; 2nd ed., 1955

——, *L'homme primitif et la religion*, Paris, 1940

Lévy-Bruhl, L., *Le surnaturel et la nature dans la mentalité primitive*, Paris, 1931

——, *La mythologie primitive*, Paris, 1935

——, *L'expérience mystique et les symboles chez les primitifs*, Paris, 1938

Lowie, R. H., *Primitive Religion*, New York, 1924

de Martino, E., *Naturalismo e storicismo nell' etnologia*, Bari, 1941

——, *Il mondo magico*, Torino, 1948

Mauss, M., and H. Hubert, *Mélanges d'histoire des religions,* Paris, 1909

Mensching, G., *Vergleichende Religionswissenschaft,* Leipzig, 1938; 2nd ed., revised, Heidelberg, 1949

————, *Allgemeine Religionsgeschichte,* Leipzig, 1940

————, *Geschichte der Religionswissenschaft,* Bonn, 1948

Mühlmann, W. E., *Geschichte der Anthropologie,* Bonn, 1948

————, "Ethnologie und Geschichte," *Studium Generale,* 1954, pp. 165-177

Otto, R., *Das Heilige,* Breslau, 1917; new ed., Munich, 1947. (*The Idea of the Holy,* London, 1923, rev. ed., 1929)

————, *Aufsätze das Numinose betreffend,* Gotha, 1923

————, W. F., *Theophania—Der Geist der altgriechischen Religion,* Hamburg, 1956

Pinard de la Boullaye, H., *L'étude comparée des religions,* 2 vols., Paris, 1922; 3rd ed., rev. and enlarged, 1929

Radcliffe-Brown, A. R., *Tabu,* Cambridge (England), 1940

Radin, P., *Gott und Mensch in der primitiven Welt,* Zurich, 1953. (*The World of Primitive Man,* New York, 1953)

Schmidt, W., *Handbuch der vergleichenden Religionsgeschichte. Ursprung und Wesen der Religion,* Münster, 1930. (See also F. Bornemann, "W. Schmidts Vorarbeiten für eine Neuauflage des Handbuchs der Religionsgeschichte," *Anthropos,* 50, 1955, pp. 937-941)

Tacchi Venturi, P., *et al., Storia delle Religioni,* 2 vols., 3rd ed., Torino, 1949

Widengren, G., *Religionens värld,* Stockholm, 1945, 2nd ed., 1953

————, "Evolutionism and the Problem of the Origin of Religion," *Ethnos,* 10, 1945, pp. 57-96

CHAPTER 1

Allcroft, A. H., *The Circle and the Cross,* I-II, London, 1927-1930

Bertling, C. T., *Vierzahl, Kreuz und Mandala in Asien*, Amsterdam, 1954

Bogoras, W., "Ideas of Space and Time in the Conception of Primitive Religion," *American Anthropologist*, N. S., 1917, pp. 205-266

Coomaraswamy, A. K., "Symbolism of the Dome," *Indian Historical Quarterly*, XIV, 1938, pp. 1-56

——, *Figures of Speech and Figures of Thought*, London, 1946

Corbin, H., "Terre céleste et corps de résurrection d'après quelques traditions iraniennes," *Eranos-Jahrbuch* XXII, 1954, pp. 97-194

Cuillandre, J., *La droite et la gauche dans les poèmes homériques*, Paris, 1941

Deffontaines, P., *Géographie et religions*, Paris, 1948

Deubner, L., "Mundus," *Hermes*, 58, 1933, pp. 276-287

Dombart, T., *Der Sakralturm. I: Zigurat*, Munich, 1920

Dumézil, G., *Rituels indo-européens à Rome*, pp. 27-43 (=*Aedes Rotunda Vestae*), Paris, 1954

Eliade, M., *The Myth of the Eternal Return*, New York, 1954, Chapters I and II

——, *Patterns in Comparative Religion*, New York, pp. 367-387

——, *Images et symboles*, Paris, 1952, pp. 33-72

Gaerte, W., "Kosmische Vorstellungen im Bilde Prähistorischer Zeit: Erdberg, Himmelsberg, Erdnabel und Weltströme," *Anthropos*, 9, 1914, pp. 956-979

Hentze, C., *Bronzegerät, Kultbauten, Religion im ältesten China der Chang-Zeit*, Antwerp, 1951

Müller, W., *Kreis und Kreuz*, Berlin, 1938

——, *Die blaue Hütte*, Wiesbaden, 1954

Mus, P., *Barabudur: Esquisse d'une histoire du bouddhisme fondée sur la critique archéologique des textes*, I-II, Hanoi, 1935

Nissen, H., *Orientatio: Studien zur Geschichte der Religion*, I-III, Berlin, 1906-1910

Ränk, G., *Die heilige Hinterecke im Hauskult der Völker Nordosteuropas und Nordasiens*, Helsinki, 1949

Roscher, W. H., "Neue Omphalosstudien," *Abh. der Königl. Sächs. Ges. d. Wiss., Phil.-hist. Klasse*, 31, 1, 1915

Sedlmayr, H., "Architektur als abbildende Kunst." *Österr. Akad. d. Wiss., Phil.-hist. Klasse, Sitzungsber.* 225/3, Vienna, 1948

———, *Die Entstehung der Kathedrale*, Zurich, 1950

Tucci, G., Mc'od rten e Ts' a-ts'a *nel Tibet Indiano ed Occidentale. Contributo allo studio dell' arte religiosa tibetano nel suo significato. Indo-Tibetica* I, Rome, 1932

———, *Il Simbolismo archittectonico dei tempi di Tibet Occidentale. Indo-Tibetica* III-IV, Rome, 1938

Weinstock, S., "Templum," *Mitt. d. Deutschen Archäol. Inst., Römische Abt.*, 45, 1930, pp. 111-123

Wensinck, A. J., *The Ideas of the Western Semites Concerning the Navel of the Earth*, Amsterdam, 1916

CHAPTER 2

SACRED TIME

Coomaraswamy, A. K., *Time and Eternity*, Ascona, 1947

Corbin, H., "Le temps cyclique dans le mazdéisme et dans l'ismaélisme," *Eranos-Jahrbuch*, XX, 1952, pp. 149-218

Culmann, O., *Christus und die Zeit*, Basel, 1946

Dumézil, G., "Temps et mythes," *Recherches philosophiques*, V, 1935-1936, pp. 235-251

Eliade, M., *The Myth of the Eternal Return*, New York, 1954, Chapters II and III

———, "Le temps et l'éternité dans la pensée indienne," *Eranos-Jahrbuch*, XX, 1951, pp. 219-252; *Images et symboles*, Paris, 1952, pp. 73-119

Goodenough, E. R., "The Evaluation of Symbols Recurrent in Time, as illustrated in Judaism," *Eranos-Jahrbuch,* XX, 1952, pp. 285-320

Leeuw, G. Van der, "Urzeit und Endzeit," *Eranos-Jahrbuch,* XVII, 1950, pp. 11-51

Marquart, J., "The Nawroz, its History and Significance," *Journal of the Cama Oriental Institute,* No. 31, Bombay, 1937, pp. 1-51

Mauss, M. and H. Hubert, "La représentation du temps dans la religion et la magie" in *Mélanges d'histoire des religions,* 1909, pp. 190-229

Mus, P., "La notion de temps réversible dans la mythologie bouddhique." *Annuaire de l'École pratique des Hautes Études, Section des Sciences Religieuses,* Melun, 1939

Nilsson, M. P., *Primitive Time Reckoning,* Lund, 1920

Pallis, S. A., *The Babylonian* akîtu *Festival,* Copenhagen, 1926

Puech, H. C., "La gnose et le temps," *Eranos-Jahrbuch,* XX, 1952, pp. 57-114

Quispel, G., "Zeit und Geschichte im antiken Christentum" *Eranos-Jahrbuch,* XX, 1952, pp. 115-140

Reuter, H., *Die Zeit. Eine religionswissenschaftliche Untersuchung, Diss.,* Bonn, 1941

Scheftelowitz, J., *Die Zeit als Schicksalsgottheit in der indischen und iranischen Religion,* Stuttgart, 1929

Wensinck, A. J., "The Semitic New Year and the Origin of Eschatology," *Acta Orientalia,* I, 1923, pp. 158-199

Werblowsky, R. J. Zwi, "Hanouca et Noël ou Judaïsme et Christianisme," *Revue de l'histoire des religions,* Jan.-Mar. 1954, pp. 30-68

Wilhelm, H., "Der Zeitbegriff im Buch der Wandlungen," *Eranos-Jahrbuch,* XX, 1952, pp. 321-349

Zimmern, H., "Zum babylonischen Neujahrsfest," 1-2, Leipzig, 1906, 1918: *Berichte über die Verhandl. d. Kgl. Sächs. Ges. d. Wiss.,* 58, 3; 70, 5

MYTHS

Baumann, H., *Schöpfung und Urzeit des Menschen im Mythus der afrikanischen Völker*, Berlin, 1936
Caillois, R., *Le mythe et l'homme*, Paris, 1938
Ehrenreich, P., *Die allgemeine Mythologie und ihre ethnologischen Grundlagen*, Leipzig, 1910
Gusdorf, G., *Mythe et métaphysique*, Paris, 1953
Hooke, S. H. (ed.), *Myth and Ritual*, London, 1934
———, *The Labyrinth*, London, 1935
Jensen, A. E., *Das religiöse Weltbild einer frühen Kultur*, Stuttgart, 1948
———, *Mythos und Kult bei Naturvölkern*, Wiesbaden, 1951
Jung, C. G., and K. Kerényi, *Einführung in das Wesen der Mythologie*, Amsterdam-Zurich, 1941
Kluckhohn, C., "Myths and Rituals. A General Theory," *Harvard Theological Review*, 35, 1942, pp. 45-79
Lévy-Bruhl, L., *La mythologie primitive. Le monde mythique des Australiens et des Papous*, Paris, 1936
Malinowski, B., *Myth in Primitive Psychology*, London, 1926
Pettazzoni, R., "Die Wahrheit des Mythos," *Paideuma*, IV, 1950, pp. 1-10
———, "Myths of Beginnings and Creation-Myths," *Essays on the History of Religion*, Leiden, 1954, pp. 24-36
Preuss, K. T., *Der religiöse Gehalt der Mythen*, Tübingen, 1933
Untersteiner, M., *La fisiologia del mito*, Milan, 1946

CHAPTER 3

Altheim, F., *Terra Mater*, Giessen, 1931
Bachofen, J. J., *Das Mutterrecht*, Basel, 1861; 3rd ed., 1948
Beirnaert, L., "La dimension mythique dans le sacramentalisme chrétien," *Eranos-Jahrbuch*, XVII, 1950, pp. 255-286
Daniélou, J., *Sacramentum futuri*, Paris, 1950

——, *Bible et liturgie*, Paris, 1951

——, *Les Saints païens de l'Ancien Testament*, Paris, 1956

Dieterich, A., *Mutter Erde*, 3rd ed., Leipzig-Berlin, 1925

Ehrenreich, P., *Die Sonne im Mythos*, Leipzig, 1915

Eliade, M., *Patterns in Comparative Religion*, New York, pp. 38-366

——, "La terre-mère et les hiérogamies cosmiques," *Eranos-Jahrbuch*, XXII, 1954, pp. 57-95 (*Mythes, rêves et mystères*, Paris, 1957, pp. 206-252)

Frazer, Sir J., *The Golden Bough*, I-XII, 3rd ed., London, 1911-1918

——, *The Worship of Nature*, I, London, 1926

Haekel, J., "Zum Problem des Mutterrechtes," *Paideuma*, V, 1953-54, pp. 298-322; 481-508

Hatt, G., "The Corn Mother in America and Indonesia," *Anthropos*, 46, 1951, pp. 853-914

Hentze, C., *Mythes et symboles lunaires*, Antwerp, 1932

Holmberg, U., "Der Baum des Lebens," Helsinki. *Annales Academiae Scientiarum Fennicae*, Series B, Vol. XVI, 1922-23

Kühn, H., "Das Problem des Urmonotheismus," Wiesbaden, *Akad. d. Wiss. u. d. Lit., Abh. d. geistes- u. sozialwiss. Klasse*, 1951, pp. 1639-1672

Mannhardt, W., *Wald- und Feldkulte*, I-II, 2nd ed., Berlin, 1904-1905

Meyer, J. J., *Trilogie altindischer Mächte und Feste der Vegetation*, I-III, Zurich-Leipzig, 1937

Nyberg, B., *Kind und Erde*, Helsinki, 1931

Pettazzoni, R., *Dio, L'Essere celeste nelle credenze dei popoli primitivi*, Rome, 1922

——, "Allwissende höchste Wesen bei primitivsten Völkern," *Archiv für Religionswissenschaft*, 29, 1930, pp. 109-129; 209-243

——, *L'onniscienza di Dio*, Turin, 1955

Schmidt, W., *Ursprung der Gottesidee*, I-XII, Münster in West-
    falen, 1926-1955

————, *Das Mutterrecht*, Vienna, 1955

Wensinck, A. J., *Tree and Bird as Cosmological Symbols in
    Western Asia*, Amsterdam, 1921

CHAPTER 4

Coomaraswamy, A. K., " 'Spiritual Paternity' and the 'Puppet-
    Complex,' " *Psychiatry*, 8, No. 3, August 1945, pp.
    25-35

Dumézil, G., *Jupiter, Mars, Quirinus*, Paris, 1941

————, *Horace et les Curiaces*, Paris, 1942

————, *Servius et la Fortune*, Paris, 1943

————, *Naissance de Rome*, Paris, 1944

————, *Naissance d'Archanges*, Paris, 1945

————, *Tarpeia*, Paris, 1947

————, *Mitra-Varuna*, 2nd ed., Paris, 1948

————, *Loki*, Paris, 1948

————, *Les Dieux des Indo-Européens*, Paris, 1952

Eliade, M., "Cosmical Homology and Yoga," *Journal of the
    Indian Society of Oriental Art*, Calcutta, 1937, pp. 188-
    203

————, "Mystère et régénération spirituelle dans les religions
    extra-européennes," *Eranos-Jahrbuch*, XXIII, 1955,
    pp. 57-98 (*Mythes, rêves, et mystères*, Paris, 1957,
    pp. 254-305)

Grassi, E., *Reisen ohne anzukommen. Südamerikanische Medi-
    tationen*, Hamburg, 1955

Hentze, C., *Tod, Auferstehung, Weltordnung. Das mythische
    Bild im ältesten China*, Zurich, 1955

Höfler, O., *Kultische Geheimbünde der Germanen*, I, Frankfurt-
    am-Main, 1934

————, *Germanisches Sakralkönigtum*, I, Munich-Cologne,
    1953

Jensen, A. E., *Beschneidung und Reifezeremonien bei Natur-völkern*, Stuttgart, 1932

Kerényi, K., *Prometheus. Das griechische Mythologem von der menschlichen Existenz*, Zurich, 1946

Loeb, E. M., *Tribal Initiation and Secret Society*. Univ. of California Publications in American Archaeology and Ethnology, 25, 3, pp. 249-288, 1929

Nyberg, H. S., *Die Religionen des alten Iran*, Leipzig, 1938

Peuckert, W. E., *Geheimkulte*, Heidelberg, 1951

Schurtz, H., *Altersklassen und Männerbünde*, Berlin, 1902

Slawik, A., "Kultische Geheimbünde des Japaner und Germanen," *Wiener Beiträge zur Kulturgeschichte und Linguistik*, IV, Vienna, 1936, pp. 675-764

de Vries, J., *Altgermanische Religionsgeschichte*, Vol. I, 2nd ed., Berlin, 1956, Vol. II, 2nd ed., Berlin, 1957

Wach, J., *Sociology of Religion*, Chicago, 1944

Webster, H., *Primitive Secret Society*, New York, 1908

Weiser, L., *Altgermanische Jünglingsweihen und Männerbünde*, Leipzig, 1927

Widengren, G., *Hochgottglaube im alten Iran*, Uppsala, 1938

——, *The King and the Tree of Life in Ancient Near Eastern Religion*, Uppsala, 1951

——, *Sakrales Königtum im Alten Testament und im Judentum*, Stuttgart, 1955

Wikander, S., *Der arische Männerbund*, Lund, 1938

——, *Vayu*, I, Uppsala, Leipzig, 1941

Wolfram, R., *Schwerttanz und Männerbund*, I-III, Kassel, 1936 ff.

——, "Weiberbünde," *Zeitschrift für Volkskunde*, 42, 1933, pp. 143 ff.

Index

Müller, M., 36 n.1, 46 n.3, 47
n.1-2, 74 n., 75 n.2, 170 n.,
226, 229-30
Mulugu, 124
mundus, 47
mysterium fascinans, 9-10
mysterium tremendum, 9-10,
121
myth, 95-104, 106, 139-40,
205-13

N

Nad'a, 35-36
Nāgas, 83
Na-khi, 83
nature as sacred, 116-21
naturism, 118, 121
nature mythology, 229-30
Narrow Gate, *see* gate as
symbol
navel of the earth, 38, 40, 44-
45, 47
Nawrōz, 78
Ndyambi, 124
Nebuchadnezzar, 48
Negritos, 125
Negroes of West Africa, 124
neo-Platonists, 223, 227
neo-Pythagoreanism, 223
Netsilik-Eskimos, 95
New Guinea, 98
New Year's ritual, 78-80, 104-
05, 147
Ngakola, 192

Nidaba, 59
Nicholas von Thverva, 40
Nineveh, 59
nirvāna, 176, 199
Njankupon, 124
Noah, 133-35
nomads, 34
noncosmic religion, 177
North American Indians, 73-
74
Num, 120
Numbakula, 33-34
numinous, the, 9
Nzame, 125

O

obstetric symbolism, 198-99
Obtala, 123
Oceania, 145
Olorun, 120, 123-24
Omahas, 170
Omphale, *see* navel of the
earth
Onesimus, 200
ontology, 42, 95
ontophany, 97, 117, 155
openings as symbols, 57
orbis terrarum, 47
oriental studies, 229
Oraons, 125
Origen, 225
Ortega y Gasset, J., 207
Osiris, 158